Also by Adrian Gostick and Chester Elton

The Orange Revolution
The Carrot Principle
The Daily Carrot Principle
The Invisible Employee
A Carrot a Day
The 24-Carrot Manager

Also by Adrian Gostick and Scott Christopher

The Levity Effect

ALL
IN

How the Best Managers Create
a Culture of Belief and Drive Big Results

Adrian Gostick
and Chester Elton

FREE PRESS
New York   London   Toronto   Sydney   New Delhi

NOTE TO READERS
Names of those identified in this book by only a first name have been changed.

*f*P

FREE PRESS
A Division of Simon & Schuster, Inc.
1230 Avenue of the Americas
New York, NY 10020

First Free Press hardcover edition April 2012

FREE PRESS and colophon are trademarks of Simon & Schuster, Inc.

For information about special discounts for bulk purchases,
please contact Simon & Schuster Special Sales at 1-866-506-1949
or business@simonandschuster.com.

The Simon & Schuster Speakers Bureau can bring authors to your live event.
For more information or to book an event contact the Simon & Schuster Speakers
Bureau at 1-866-248-3049 or visit our website at www.simonspeakers.com.

Manufactured in the United States of America

7   9   10   8

Library of Congress Cataloging-in-Publication Data

Gostick, Adrian Robert.
All in : how the best managers create a culture of belief and drive big results /
by Adrian Gostick & Chester Elton.
p. cm.
1. Organizational behavior. 2. Corporate culture. 3. Employee motivation.
I. Elton, Chester. II. Title.
HD58.7.G673 2012
658.3'14—dc23 2011045590

ISBN 978-1-4516-5982-5
ISBN 978-1-4516-5984-9 (ebook)

Not long ago we embarked on an exciting journey. What we've been able to accomplish independently would never have been possible without the support of so many dear friends that if we tried to list them it would fill most of the book. We thank you all.

We dedicate this book to those who give us their undying love and support, our families. Jennifer and Tony, and Heidi, Cassi, Carter, Brinden, and Garrett—you believed in us and our work and have never wavered in your belief that we could make a difference in the world. Your love sustains us; together we are all in.

Contents

PART III.
Culture Tools:
Dealing with Challenges;
Ideas to Maintain Success

PART I

Culture Works

The One Thing That Differentiates Your Team and Drives Real Results

1

Get in the Wheelbarrow

Why Aren't They Giving Their All?

Some twenty-five thousand onlookers had turned out on June 30, 1859, as a flamboyant, mustached Frenchman known as the Great Blondin stepped out onto a three-inch cord that stretched across roaring Niagara Falls. They were in high spirits, curious to see if the daredevil would become the first person to cross the chasm on a tightrope or if he would plummet to his death. Either way it would be a day to remember.

Blondin had been born as Jean-François Gravelet and had been an acrobat since childhood, raised in the circus tents of Europe. He knew his craft, and the showman had no doubt he would be successful. It was not bravado; it was merely something he took to be a fact—as true as the sky being blue. And, as history shows, he not only crossed the fifteen-hundred-foot-wide falls without a stumble but even paused to perform a back somersault on his return trip. The breathless crowd erupted into wild cheers when he set his feet on firm ground.

The Great Blondin would cross the gorge eight times over the next decade, all with theatrical variations—blindfolded, on stilts, but most often trundling a small wheelbarrow. As you can imagine, crowds flocked to see him and he began to draw loyal devotees. According to accounts, the mob on one summer day was especially boisterous, and they gave him a chorus of hurrahs as he approached pushing his familiar barrow.

"Do you believe I can cross the falls with this wheelbarrow?" he called out.

"Yes!" they yelled as one.

"Wonderful," he said. "Then who will get in?"

Many in the crowd laughed but then fell silent as they realized he wasn't joking. Blondin waited as the seconds ticked by; a haze of gray cigar smoke hung just above their heads. They stood awkward and immobile. There were no takers. Blondin had hoped his fans would believe, as he did, in his infallible prowess on the high wire. They said they did, but they really didn't.

Then someone did. Blondin's agent, Harry Colcord, took off his silk top hat and waved it high above his head. He was volunteering.

Blondin was greatly moved by the gesture. Despite the drama of the day, he actually hadn't intended to wheel anyone across the falls, but Colcord's offer sparked an idea. Instead of pushing his agent then, he returned a few months later and carried Colcord across the falls on his shoulders, an amazing feat considering the man was only a few pounds lighter than the showman.

Let's stop there. This book is clearly not about daredevils or tightrope walkers, but about a related drama that is taking place in organizations every day, all around the world. While most managers by now understand that their most reliable competitive advantage comes from their people, few of them actually know how to get people "all in"—convincing employees to truly buy into their ideas and the strategy they've put forward, to give that extra push that leads to outstanding results.

It's not for lack of effort. Most leaders we meet seem to be bending over backward for their people. They walk the floor, listen respectfully to their employees' ideas, and try to be accommodating. They've been taught they need to be people managers, not slaves to process, and as a result they're focusing more, one-on-one, on the needs of each person in their care.

And yet overall performance isn't improving, or not nearly enough.

This is backed up by the data we see. Employee engagement

scores haven't improved much at most organizations after many years of effort, and companies aren't seeing markedly greater amounts of innovation or employee initiative. As hard as managers have been working, something's missing: It's culture.

Whether you manage the smallest of teams or a multicontinent organization, you are the proud owner of a culture—congratulations—and it's important to understand that the effectiveness of that culture will have a big impact on your performance. If your culture is clear, positive, and strong, then your people will buy into your ideas and cause and, most important, will believe what they do matters and that they can make a difference. That pervasive enthusiasm and energy will spread like perfume in the atmosphere. On the other hand, if your culture is dysfunctional—chaotic, combative, or indifferent—employees will most likely spend more time thinking about why the people sitting next to them should be fired than getting fired up themselves.

Now, a reader might ask why the carrot guys are writing a book on culture. The answer is simple: We've worked with clients on leadership issues for almost twenty years now, and hardly a week has gone by that we haven't excitedly called each other to talk about a fascinating corporate culture we've just stumbled upon. For a long time we've believed that culture is what makes teams and organizations great, and yet no one was talking about it in popular business literature and it seemed that no one really wanted to. Perhaps culture seemed the sole purview of CEOs and human resource departments. Unquestionably the boss of a small IT department or regional call center wouldn't have the audacity to claim he had a culture, right?

But over the last few years something has changed. As we meet with new clients, expecting them to want us to work with them on the more focused ideas of employee recognition or teamwork, the subjects of our two last books, they keep steering the conversation back to culture. And not just their overall corporate culture; they have awoken to the fact that if the culture in their Cincinnati office isn't working, then no amount of thankyous or esprit de corps will help.

They have learned that if a culture works, then everything works better.

Take the case of Andrew Heath, who when we met him was the newly appointed president of the energy business of Rolls-Royce, one of the four sectors of the iconic British firm. Heath's face lit up as he described a business improvement team of seventy people he had led years before in the company's aerospace business. With more work than the team could reasonably achieve, he knew he needed to create a "special environment" where people would truly care about the success of the venture. He needed more than discretionary effort; he needed to create a culture "where employees would see the problem before them as a challenge rather than as something to drag them down."

Heath realized he couldn't achieve the assigned goals by force of character alone. He needed to change his leadership style and engage the whole team by asking them what they thought would increase their commitment to the job, what help they needed, and what would give them greater satisfaction. They came up with ideas to pair new employees with senior people, identify training needs, present above-and-beyond awards for great work (a favorite became bottles of champagne), hold regular update luncheons, and so on. Unassuming things, really, but the outcome was not only increased employee ownership and dramatic business results but also a level of camaraderie that is rare.

"We achieved more than we thought possible. The team and I had never worked so hard in our lives. It was a tough assignment, but we had such fun in the process," Heath said. "I knew we had created a special culture together, but it only really struck me how much impact it had on the individual team members when we got together for a reunion a few years later. Everyone spoke of the profound effect it had had on their subsequent leadership styles."

Savvy leaders like Heath realize it is culture that will differentiate your team or organization and drive real business results.

John F. W. Rogers, distinguished partner of the investment banking firm Goldman Sachs, put his finger on the crucial role of culture when he said, "Our bankers travel on the same planes as our competitors. We stay at the same hotels. In a lot of cases, we have the same clients as our competition. So when it comes down to it, it is a combination of the execution and culture that makes the difference between us and other firms. That's why our culture is necessary—it's the glue that binds us together."

Those words stuck with us and bear repeating: Culture is the difference; it is the glue that binds us together.

Over the years we've been asked to work with some pretty impressive organizations all over the globe, including American Express, the National Football League, Cigna, the U.S. Army, Rolls-Royce, and Johnson & Johnson, to drop a few names. It's probably no surprise we found great cultures in those places. And yet we have found similarly amazing places to work in every industry we've studied—even in workplaces where you might not expect culture to thrive or make a difference.

Consider this example. A few years ago we were asked to conduct a workshop at Crothall Healthcare. With thirty thousand employees, this is one of the largest and fastest-growing companies you've probably never heard of. They clean hospitals and offices, maintain facilities, transport patients, process linens, and so on. It's not sexy stuff, but stick with us on this. Every five years Crothall doubles in size. At less than twenty years old, the company has annual revenues in excess of a billion dollars—which is a heck of a lot more than we were making when we were twenty!

We were halfway through our presentation to the senior leadership team, and just about to reach the crux of our argument, when the chief executive officer, Bobby Kutteh, made a mad dash for the door. It was disappointing but not unexpected; CEOs are, after all, in demand. But less than thirty seconds elapsed before he returned, reached up to the stage, and handed us bottles of water. He'd heard our voices were getting dry after talking for so long in the hot auditorium, so he'd raced to the lobby to find us a drink.

We've been doing this for a long time. Let us count for you the number of times this has happened before . . . zero.

We appreciated the gesture and it made us think well of Kutteh, but we also realized that the moment was bigger than that. He was exemplifying the culture of Crothall. His act reinforced what didn't need to be spoken: Crothall is a caring place. Indeed, we found the act was utterly symbolic of the kind of overall corporate culture that Kutteh and his leadership team have created. It is a humble, sincere, service-oriented environment. And as you could rightly infer from that simple action of running to get us a drink, Kutteh is a servant to his people. It's one reason he's loved. Yes, loved. Just about everyone who was in the audience that day would do just about anything for this guy.

Before we spoke, Kutteh had talked for forty-five minutes. He addressed the audience without notes, with just a lavalier microphone affixed to his button-down shirt, sleeves rolled up. As he paced back and forth he outlined the strategy for the future, cracked jokes, thanked his leaders, and asked everyone to walk a little taller by taking better care of their employees.

"My dad used to say people will always remember how you make them feel," he said. "A little stroke of kindness to your employees can go a long way." And when he was done, every one of the two hundred and thirty leaders stood—no, they jumped to their feet and gave him a standing ovation that lasted and lasted. It was a fantastic moment.

You don't have to look any farther than this very unassuming, very successful hospital-cleaning company to see that culture works.

But the fact is there is still nowhere near enough emphasis on culture. Business schools and leadership books teach us the mechanics of processes—strategy, marketing and product development, supply-chain management, playing to our strengths, even choosing the right employees. All are important, without a doubt. But as counterintuitive as it may sound to some, the thing that sets you apart from your peers is rarely what you sell or how you package or promote it. You all look pretty similar to us consumers. No, unless you've just invented the iPod of your industry, it's likely that your competitors offer, more or less, the same things you do at about the same prices. The secret of moving a business forward is in getting your working population to differentiate you.

As Stephen Sadove, chairman and chief executive officer of department store giant Saks Incorporated, said, "When I talk to Wall Street, people really want to know your results, what are your strategies, what are the issues, and what is it that you're doing to drive your business. Never do you get people asking about the culture." But, he concluded, it is culture that drives "whatever you are trying to accomplish within a company—innovation, execution, whatever it's going to be. And that then drives results."

Sadove knows that if a culture works, then everything else works better. And we've discovered that it works a *whole lot* better, with the help of some powerful research we'll unveil in this book.

And yet if you've worked in enough jobs, you'll know that cultures can vary dramatically. There are workplaces of outright dysfunction, of contention, of coasting, and even of backstabbing. There are some cultures that produce impressive financial results but also high employee turnover and burnout. As a professional told us in a consumer products company, "Around here they put a gun in your back on day one. The trigger is pulled, and if you stop running the bullet is going to get you." We could go on, of course, describing the varieties, but you get the point. What we will show in this book is that the most profitable, productive, enduring cultures are places where people lock into a vision with conviction, where they maintain excitement not out of fear but out of passion. They are cultures where people believe.

A number of compelling studies, going back many years, have shown that such a positive culture is a key driver of results. Exhibit A is a study done in the mid-1990s by Harvard Business School professors John Kotter and James Heskett. They followed two hundred companies to learn if a positive culture—one that facilitated adaptation to a changing world and that highly valued employees—really affected a firm's long-term economic performance. The results were staggering. They found that those strong cultures "encourage leadership from everyone in the firm. So if customer needs change, a firm's culture almost forces people to change their practices to meet the new needs. And anyone, not just a few people, is empowered to do just that."

The financial impact of such a culture? Over the eleven-year period studied by the professors, revenue growth in the companies with "positive" cultures grew an average of 682 percent compared with 166 percent in the firms with "weak" cultures, and the difference between stock appreciation was 901 percent to 74 percent. Astounding.

But, you might ask, can a strong culture make a measurable difference in a team or division? Enter Exhibit B, a field study conducted in 2001 by the University of California at Los Angeles's Eric Flamholtz. The UCLA professor studied a midsize industrial firm with twenty divisions all doing fairly similar work. He found the departments that behaved in ways most consistent with the company's desired culture had markedly better financial performance—whereas the lower-performing divisions did not have cultural buy-in. The findings for this $800 million firm were so striking that "effective culture management" was immediately added to every manager's performance management system and bonus calculation.

Okay, so we see team buy-in to culture makes a difference, but can a single manager really influence a culture to that great a degree? Absolutely. In fact, the level of impact might shock you. As we'll demonstrate through both research and stories of exceptional managers we've observed closely, you as the manager are the core influencer of the kind of culture at play in your team, division, or whole company.

If you're incredulous about your influence, you are not the only one. In our consulting work we are often faced with quantifying how much sway managers really have over performance. Sometimes leaders doubt if it is in their power to influence morale, productivity, and profitability. They know some work groups perform better than others, but it is difficult to pinpoint the exact reasons why and even a little uncomfortable to wonder if it is within their power to shape success.

So consider this. Recently, we worked with a health care system in the San Francisco area that had embarked on an experiment to investigate this long-standing business dilemma of the effect of a manager on performance. The organization started by classifying each department within their hospitals as green, yellow, or red. Green departments were terrific places to work. They had not only higher-than-normal team productivity and profitability but also great employee engagement scores and better-than-average employee retention. They were the kind of work groups we all want to be a part of, so workers came and stayed.

In contrast, yellow departments had average employee survey scores. They weren't bad teams but they weren't great.

As you might imagine, red departments were poor on every metric, especially employee turnover. It seemed workers couldn't get out of the red work groups fast enough.

Then the organization conducted an interesting experiment. They moved quite a number of managers of green departments to red departments, and managers of red work groups were asked to lead green workplaces. They imagined that this shuffle would show whether leadership really mattered. What happened? The head of HR shook her head and said, "In every single case—every case—no matter the background or expertise of the manager, within a year the red departments were green and green departments had turned red. It was the manager who made the difference."

Our decision to focus in this book on *how* managers can make a difference in a culture was inspired by yet another piece of powerful research, which we worked on with Towers Watson, one of the most respected names in global research and professional services. Together we created the parameters of how to communicate the results of a major new study that showed the way the most profitable companies work—on the inside. This breakthrough information became a vital part of this book. From its eight-million-person global database collected during 2009 and 2010 alone from 700 companies, Towers Watson identified 25 companies with a total of 303,000 employees that enjoyed high-performance business results—organizations that outperformed their competitors in financial measures by as much as two and three times. This Global High-Performance list includes a thin slice of the best of the best—companies from around the world and in every industry: health care, financial services, manufacturing, high tech, services, transportation, and so on.

The task in the study was to determine what levers managers of these organizations pulled to bring about such dramatically better financial results than their peers and how they did it during the abysmal market conditions we experienced during the last few years. We will introduce the discoveries from this study more fully in chapter 3, but the core finding was that in the highest-performing cultures, leaders not only create high levels of *engagement*—manifest in strong employee attachment to the company and a willingness to give extra effort—but they also create environments that support productivity and performance, in which employees feel *enabled*. And finally, they help employees feel a greater sense of well-being and drive at work; in other words, people feel *energized*.

This triumvirate of engaged, enabled, and energized (E + E + E for short)—integrated into a single measurement and approach by Towers Watson—was found in every highly profitable culture studied. It's a unique combination that can boost any company, division, or small team to new heights.

To grasp the substantial impact of the three Es on pecuniary results, take a glance at the chart on the next page. The financial results of the Global High-Performance companies (the ones that enjoy high levels of each E + E + E) are compared with a group of companies with only high employee engagement as well as a group with low engagement scores. The research shows the cumulative effect of the three Es at work. The engaged, enabled, and energized cultures saw average annual operating margins of 27.4 percent during a period that included a recession/ economic downturn—twice as high as organizations with just high employee engagement and three times higher than those with low engagement scores.

As a primer, operating margin is the percentage of a company's sales left over after it pays for wages, raw materials, and other costs; it essentially gives investors an idea of how much profit you really make on each dollar of sales, before interest and taxes. For instance, an operating margin of 9.9 percent means that a company makes just under ten cents—before interest and taxes—on every buck it earns; pretty slim. The higher the margin, the more profitable the company. Operating margins above 27 percent are rare and worthy of exploration. They indicate efficiently run organizations, but also ones where customers are willing to pay a premium for their services.

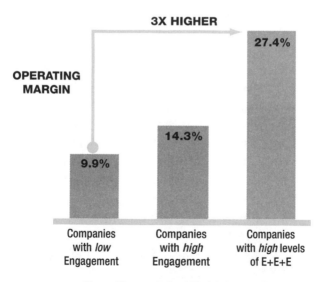

Towers Watson study of 50 global companies.

Over the past twenty years we had met some pretty cool managers in some cool companies, but that wasn't enough to make a case. This data on E + E + E was, and we began sharing it.

It seemed to resonate with people. Heads were nodding. However, we quickly met resistance. As the manager of a bank in New York said to us, "Okay, your research is solid. Your models make sense." We smiled gratefully, and then he continued. "I get it, culture is important, and I see what it looks like from your findings. What I want to know is *how* to do it. I do . . . *what, exactly?*"

I do what? It was a superbly well-placed question. Of course he had every right to know not only what makes a culture great but also the steps he must take to get there—to bond people to his ideas and his cause and make his culture really work. As Alice might say, his straightforward question made us "curiouser and curiouser," and our curiosity became an obsession—how do regular managers build amazing cultures where people buy enthusiastically into goals and visions, where they deliver top-shelf service and ingenuity?

The fact is most managers have little notion how to create a culture in their team—or even how to put into words what they are looking for. As we ask managers about their specific team cultures, we are often told that they have a strong one, but that it's hard to define. Sorry for being blunt, but that's rubbish. If it's so excruciatingly hard to describe your culture, then you don't have a great one. Culture isn't invisible, indefinable. When you walk into a great culture, it smacks you in the face with its concreteness. We've all experienced this firsthand. There is a tangible feeling about spending time in an Apple store where employees are truly enabled to meet your needs, or phoning Zappos and sharing a laugh with an energized customer service agent, or having a cup of coffee at a really hip Starbucks. It is an atmosphere that engulfs you immediately and lingers with you after you leave.

In this book we will answer the two most overlooked business questions of our day: Why is it that some work cultures get their people to buy in wholeheartedly and others don't? And what can managers of any level do to build and sustain profitable, vibrant cultures of their own?

≈ ALL IN ≈

THE SEVEN-STEP ROAD MAP

On a Monday not long ago a friend left us a voice mail. He is one of the most talented marketing professionals we know, but after years of feeling dissed by his boss he had become disengaged at work. What follows is the transcript of the message:

> *It's ten twenty-four and I'm driving in to work. [pause] That's right, ten twenty-four. Business as usual. And it just . . . doesn't . . . matter. [sarcastically] But I'm committed. You can call me a workaholic, you can call me a chocoholic, but doggone it I will be there at the crack of eleven every day, making sure that the three point five hours I put in drumming on my desk with my pencils like George Costanza working on the Penske account . . . remember that episode? . . .*

He trailed off without finishing the thought. It would have been funny if it weren't so haunting. Talent wasted.

Our friend may be an extreme case, but almost every manager today is dealing with a good deal of disillusionment and disengagement of some kind or other. Despite all the hard work bosses have invested in recent years to seem caring and attentive, statistics show that workers aren't buying it. The average employee spends about fifteen hours a month complaining about his or her manager. That's basically twenty-four days a year, a full month of workdays, grumbling and getting nothing done. Right now employee teams and entire organizational cultures around the world are crumbling from misunderstanding and neglect. It is a crippling crisis of belief, and the symptom is what many we've spoken to in the military refer to as "retired on active duty." Consider these sobering statistics: As of 2010, according to the Gallup Organization, 52 percent of employees were not engaged at work and 18 percent were so disengaged that they were regularly working against their organization's goals. Indeed, most leaders we speak with feel like their employees are losing their drive, energy, and focus on results.

It takes a concerted effort to reengage people. We wish we could tell you it will be easy, but of course, it takes work. The process we will introduce you to will require that you take some time away from your clients, from your deliverables. It will force you to become a coach and no longer a player. But the results are exponential as you learn to harness the full power of all the people in your care.

What we introduce in this book is a manager's practical guide to developing a robust culture where people buy in. The road map we will present is based on in-depth research and long experience working with executives and managers at leading companies. You'll see that the tactical tools a leader uses to build a strong culture include some timeless principles of management but also new ideas that emerged from our studies.

Here, in capsule form, is an overview of the steps we've found have the most powerful effect:

Define your burning platform. Employees typically don't buy into a way of doing business without clear and compelling reasons, and yet most leaders provide little or no justification as they introduce their ideas and strategies and ask their people for improved results. In the best workplaces, though, leaders define the mission with great clarity and instill a sense of urgency, making it clear that if they don't all do their utmost to carry it through, before long they will find themselves on the precipice of calamities. We introduce the best methods for creating this clarity of mission and developing the resolve to achieve it.

Create a customer focus. In the highest-performing cultures, managers convey that employees must focus like lasers on customers, and they mandate a vigorous pro-customer orientation. This not only leads to exceptionally high client satisfaction and loyalty, but it provides moment-to-moment direction for all employees in making the right decisions and taking initiative on their own.

Develop agility. When we initiated this research, it shocked us to find the concept of agility arising as one of the top handful of management skills in high-performance cultures. This hadn't shown up on leadership studies we had conducted even a few years ago, but we're in a world of increasingly rapid change and uncertainty, and this recent research has shown that the top-performing companies are seen by both their employees and their customers as much more able to deal with change. Employees are more insistent than ever that their managers see into the future and do a decent job of addressing the coming challenges and capitalizing on new opportunities.

Share everything. The best cultures are places of truth, of constant communication, and of marked transparency. Managers in these cultures share even the hard truths with their employees as soon as they can, and they encourage debate even if it rattles harmony. They leave the "pillows" at home; in other words, they don't soften the blows. Employees know that their managers will be truthful and direct, and that builds trust and a larger culture of openness.

Partner with your talent. Great managers think differently about their employees. They believe their success is a direct result of their peoples' unique ingenuity and talent, not their own brilliance. As a result, they treat people like true partners and have a sincere desire to create opportunities for them to grow and develop—thereby retaining the best. This notion for some leaders is akin to fingernails on a chalkboard, but before employees will buy into a culture, they must be able to answer the WIIFM question: "What's in it for me?"

Root for each other. "In the most innovative companies, there is a significantly higher volume of thank-yous than in companies of low innovation," says Rosabeth Moss Kanter of Harvard Business School. Given our background in recognition, we were thrilled to find higher levels of appreciation and camaraderie in not only the innovative places we studied, but in cultures of great customer service, operational excellence, compassion, and ownership. In the best workplaces, teammates had much higher levels of goodwill and they spent much more time thanking each other peer-to-peer. These seemingly warm and fuzzy skills created tangible esprit de corps and a single-mindedness about living the right behaviors.

Establish clear accountability. As a capstone to this process, managers must learn how to hold employees accountable—and yet they must turn this idea from a negative into a positive. Employees want to be held accountable for hitting their goals, but they must be given the responsibility and tools to ensure their success, and then rewarded when they see a goal through to completion.

As we'll show in part 2 of this book, each of these components builds upon the others, and each is a necessary element of a successful culture. We hope our presentation of how each can be enhanced will help you identify core changes you can make that will result in dramatic improvements. As you'll see, small adjustments in direction now can lead to big improvements.

Take this case of how one talented leader made remarkable headway by establishing more accountability. Soon after Margie Lynch took over as divisional vice president of talent and human capital services at Kmart, the number three discount retailer in the United States, she went on a yearlong tour of the entire format teaching district mangers how to set goals and then hold themselves and their associates accountable.

"I kept hearing people describe others in our culture with terms like 'She's so nice.' That was fine, but I wanted to hear things like 'She's so nice, and wow, she gets a lot done.'"

Kmart had a friendly culture, but what they needed was a culture of friendliness combined with healthy levels of follow-up.

Managers needed to learn that accountability wasn't a negative, it was part of the vital process of being open with each other, of building trust. And the result of many cultural-improvement efforts in this 100,000-person organization? Kmart is not only gaining some serious buzz as a great place to work in retail but is beating its largest competitor, Walmart, in same-store sales. A pretty remarkable turnaround considering the very public challenges Kmart has faced in its history.

As you'll see in the chapters to come this is a book about culture, but more so it is the story of how great leaders create unique, inviting, and profitable places to work. Today's successful business leaders are less the tyrannical symphony conductor or decisive military genius of yesteryear, but they also haven't bent over so far backward in their sensitivity that they've lost their focus. They are more Dr. Martin Luther King Jr. than George Patton, more Mother Teresa than Karl Marx. The modern leader provides the why, keeps an ear close to those they serve, is agile and open, treats their people with deference, and creates a place where every step forward is noted and applauded.

The questions will we answer are these: How do you create an emotional connection with your employees that can transform their passive curiosity into Harry Colcord–like faith? How do you influence others to "get in the wheelbarrow"?

Right now you may be facing indifference or resistance. Your particular situation may seem impossible, inexorable. It is not. There is a path to a hidden reservoir of drive and dedication in your people. There is a process by which seeds of a strong culture can begin to grow.

As you'll see, the era of survival is over; the age of belief is upon us.

2

The Belief Factor

The Secret Sauce That Makes a Culture Contagious

You'd think it would be easy to get people to believe at work. After all, for thousands of years, our species has searched for meaning in being part of something bigger than ourselves. It is part of the human condition; we all want to be a contributing part of a community—whether civic, religious, ethnic, political, or social. We all strive to believe in something.

At work, we organize people into communities. We give them important roles. Heck, we pay them—even on days when they stay home sick in bed.

Then why don't they believe?

It would be a mistake to think that people will commit to a work culture because of a mandate. You can't influence belief by wielding your title and power or even sending well-worded missives. We can just see the memo now: "Starting next Tuesday, you will believe everything we say." No, belief at work is a choice, and the first step to becoming a leader who can influence others to believe is to do something very un-manager-like: pause and think about human nature. Why do people believe in the things they do? And how can they be persuaded to change what they think?

Every person who works for you has arrived in your employ

with his or her own set of theories about the world, most often shaded by experiences that have hardened their resolve or even created built-in resistance. You see, belief is a double-edged sword. On the positive side, it can be a force for inconceivable, blow-the-doors-off achievement. Negative beliefs, however, or even simple skepticism, can be enormous impediments to the success of any culture.

It takes skill and time to turn negative beliefs into positive. But too many managers we work with are averse to the very notion that employee belief must be earned. They argue, *Hey, the checks are clearing, what right do they have not to buy in?* It seems logical that their people should be in alignment with them because they have the office with the most ceiling tiles (a measure used by one company we visited to gauge a manager's importance). But ceiling tiles and a fancy job title do not guarantee that people will commit to you—at least, not in a way that garners high performance.

The bottom line is this: Leaders too often ask their people to agree with the strategies, policies, and goals of their culture without really knowing how to persuade them. We have seen this problem in every industry and on every continent.

Unfortunately, many well-meaning but busy leaders have a tendency, whether managing two people or two thousand, to see workers from a distance, like the Great Blondin looking down from his perch over the falls. They imagine that because people report to them they are one with them, that while employees might not quite love them, they at least respect them and believe that they are sensible and well-intentioned. The problem is, that's just not a reasonable assumption.

Yes, it is a safe bet to say that some of your employees are completely on board with you, but it's just as safe to say that many are either skeptical about your leadership or view things with a detached indifference. The Great Blondin had fans, but they all chose to stay on safe ground. A certain portion even watched with the hope he would fail and fall. It is not unreasonable that some of your workers have a similar morbid curiosity about the potential of your failure. *Get in the wheelbarrow? I don't think so.*

The fact is, even the more earnest of your people have difficulty buying into everything you are selling; they are well aware that your misstep could mean trouble for them. That idea is worth repeating: Given that failure could cost them their future security, why shouldn't they be at least a little dubious about your initiatives? The message is clear: We have become a free-agent nation. People may join companies or brands, but they quit their bosses—either literally or by withholding belief, which leads to diminished effort.

Honestly, you shouldn't blame your people for being jaded. Many of them have been disappointed by prior leaders, or maybe they've invested lots of time in some big new initiative that complicated their lives only to see it fizzle or implode. Leaders all too seldom take into account the risks inherent in their propositions from the point of view of their employees or understand the reasons why employees may be resistant.

It's not that people don't want to believe in their managers. They do. Whether you work in a retail store or bank, hospital or high-tech cube maze, working for a company and a manager you believe in is a lot more satisfying than just cashing a paycheck. It's why we've seen such a proliferation of interest in mission-driven nonprofits in recent years. Teach for America, for instance, places recent college graduates as instructors in low-income schools for a two-year term. That organization alone has seen a tenfold increase in applicants and placements over the past decade. Why? Because we all want to believe that we are making a difference.

It reminds us of a recent conversation with an old friend who after more than two decades working in corporate America told us, "I've come to realize I want a noble cause, not just a paycheck." He is a part of a generation's search to belong to something meaningful.

That's a need that goes back a long, long time.

Picture a prehistoric hunter, gruff and shaggy, digging a shallow hole on a cold morning to bury his clan mate. In the grave he places a few tools, an ax, some clothing, and a pouch with berries and dried venison. Anthropologists have uncovered Paleolithic grave sites such as this scattered across Europe and Asia, but they don't make sense. What's to be gained by throwing away good food and valuable tools? Why would undeveloped Neanderthals bury their dead with such ceremony? The best educated guess is this: Early man wanted to help the departed meet whatever adventures lay ahead on the other side with weapons and food. It seems Neanderthals had devised a system of thinking that assured them that death could be survived. They had come to trust that their world was not chaotic but governed by a powerful force that one could appeal to through pragmatic measures. This suggests that as soon as early men began to behave like human beings, they began to wonder about the mysteries of existence, to try to make sense of the world around them and form their own beliefs.

And the point for us in business? Beliefs are intimately woven with human biology, and our biology compels us and allows us to have beliefs. Says psychological researcher Andrew Newberg, who has done pioneering work in brain science and belief, "The involuntary mental drive is the cognitive imperative; it is the almost irresistible, biologically driven need to make sense of things."

So, why aren't our people trying to make sense of what we, their leaders, are telling them at work? Why don't they lock onto the core messages of the culture and believe? Because it's also true that over those thousands of years our species has developed natural inclinations to hold tight to preconceptions and to have a set of biases that entrench us in what we think is right, even despite evidence to the contrary.

Thus, before we can understand how to get people to buy into our culture, we should understand the reasons behind why they come to believe, or fail to, and then how we can influence a change in those beliefs. That means learning just enough social psychology to know that a good portion of the people in our charge will naturally resist us, doubting our ability to lead them, actively struggling against any new direction, or indifferently ignoring our pleas.

As we'll show, a great deal has been discovered in the last few decades about why people hold the beliefs they do, and one of the most fundamental findings, emerging in study after study, is that we cling to our beliefs, right or wrong.

≈ ALL IN ≈

FROM SADDAM HUSSEIN TO PLATO

By the fall of 2004, a year and a half after the U.S. invasion of Iraq, a majority of people in the United States still refused to admit they were wrong about why the United States was there. Some 72 percent of voting Americans believed that Saddam Hussein, the former president of that Middle Eastern country, had directly or indirectly helped bring down the Twin Towers in New York City on September 11, 2001. This was despite overwhelming evidence to the contrary. The 9/11 Commission had found no link, and President George W. Bush himself had denied the connection.

Why would people hold steadfastly to the idea that Saddam was linked to these terrorist attacks?

A group of psychological researchers from Northwestern, the University of North Carolina, and the State University of New York offer a powerful explanation: We engage in what is called *motivated reasoning*. "Rather than search rationally for information that either confirms or disconfirms a particular belief, people actually seek out information that *endorses* what they *already* believe," said one of those academics, Steve Hoffman. Our mistaken belief is not caused by the absence of correct information (there was plenty of that around on this point), but by our tendency to seek out and put our faith in information that supports the belief we're predisposed to. We have an intransigent *unwillingness* to believe contradictory information or change our opinions, and will even engage in elaborate rationalizations to provide alternative explanations for the solid evidence against what we'd thought.

As part of this research, the professors conducted one-on-one "challenge interviews" with forty-nine people who still believed the Saddam-involvement theory after it was disproved. The interviews lasted as long as two hours. Even after showing these individuals newspaper articles quoting President Bush, forty-eight of the forty-nine stuck to their guns.

This isn't a matter of being a fanatic. Many of the forty-nine individuals Hoffman and his colleagues interviewed were rational men and women who felt fundamentally that Saddam was a madman and a threat to the security of the free world, and that it was only a matter of time before the U.S. would have to deal with him again (they plausibly cited Iraq's invasion of Kuwait as an example). The fact that half the country voted for President Bush in the 2000 and 2004 elections shows that tens of millions of people supported the commander in chief and wanted to find evidence that his administration was making wise choices. (PS: Please don't send us a nasty e-mail accusing us of bashing one political party. This important point is larger than politics. We could be citing high levels of such motivated reasoning that researchers found regarding the behavior of Democratic president Bill Clinton during the Monica Lewinsky scandal. This data about Iraq is simply more current.)

The subconscious nature of motivated reasoning makes it hard to catch yourself doing it. Think about a big, controversial idea that's been the subject of public discussion: nationalizing health care, global warming, or legalizing marijuana are a few that immediately get just about everyone talking. Now think about the so-called experts who are booked on news shows to debate the merits of various pieces of information. How often have you seen one of these people stop in midsentence after strong evidence is presented, carefully consider his opponent's argument, and change his tune? Most likely your answer is, *Yeah, I've never seen that.*

The theory of motivated reasoning identifies a number of the

ways in which resistance manifests itself, which you will almost
surely recognize in employee reactions to your efforts to persuade them:

- **Counter-arguing.** Employees, out loud, or more likely behind
  your back, will directly rebut the new way of thinking or acting with "Yeah, but . . ." statements that discredit the new
  information or the source (you).
- **Attitude bolstering.** They will bring up facts that support
  their current position without directly refuting or even considering the new way of being.
- **Selective exposure.** Despite your best efforts to reach them
  through various mediums, workers will ignore or avoid new
  information completely.
- **Disputing rationality.** Some will finally resort to the argument
  that their opinions do not need to be grounded in facts with
  statements such as "I can still have my opinion, can't I?"

And yet the most pernicious method by which our brains
cling to our beliefs is something called *inferred justification.*
This is particularly fascinating to us, because it can work both
ways for managers. Inferred justification is a process by which
people actually invent the causal links necessary to justify their
belief or behavior. In other words, people simply *assume* that
there is evidence to support their belief. Now, in some cases this
theory works to the benefit of managers of highly committed
cultures, as employees who are engaged and satisfied will infer
their leaders are doing the right things and will pay close attention when they speak, take notes and nod thoughtfully, and actually do what is asked of them. Unfortunately, though, those who
feel at least somewhat disengaged—about 40 percent in most
companies—will invent justifications for continuing to feel that
way, no matter what management is doing to improve the situation. And these people don't just keep their opinions to themselves. They become, to various degrees, counterrevolutionaries
who recruit others to join their state of dissatisfaction.

Why do our minds work this way? One reason is that we have an unconscious impulse to relieve mental tension—or what's called cognitive dissonance—when we are presented with information that contradicts what we think is right. Plato captured this brilliantly around 380 BC in his epic work *The Republic*. He asked his readers to imagine a cave inhabited by prisoners who have been chained immobile since childhood, compelled to gaze at a wall in front of them. Behind the prisoners is an enormous fire, and between the fire and the prisoners is a walkway where people carry things on their heads, including figures of animals made of wood and stone.

The prisoners watch the shadows cast by the firelight and the figures, but they do not know they are shadows. The images are their reality.

Now suppose a prisoner is freed, said Plato. If someone were to show him the things that had cast the shadows—a stone lion or a wooden bear—he would not recognize them; he would believe the shadows on the wall were more real than what he was seeing. "Wouldn't he try to turn his gaze back toward the shadows, as toward what he can see clearly and hold to be real?" asked the philosopher. "What if someone forcibly dragged such a man upward, out of the cave: wouldn't the man be angry at the one doing this to him?"

That was 2,400 years ago, and yet Plato identified one of the main problems facing modern business leaders. When managers come up with a new initiative or ask their employees to do things a certain way, many of their people are internally irritated and a few resentful. The only thing that will change them is what Plato called a "rebirth of perception." Then, after that awakening, the philosopher explained, "wouldn't [the former prisoner] remember his first home, what passed for wisdom there, and his fellow prisoners, and consider himself happy and them pitiable? Wouldn't he disdain whatever honors, praises, and prizes were awarded there to the ones who guessed best which shadows followed which?"

So, how to facilitate such a rebirth? Is there hope with all of that natural inclination for employees to resist believing in you and your goals? Do you really have a chance to bring them around?

Unquestionably. And we discovered some fascinating research about the process conducted by a former psychologist who now works with executive teams and members of C-suites to address the psychological aspects of getting people to buy in.

≈ ALL IN ≈

WOULD OIL WORKERS EAT TOFU?

In the fall of 2007 Dr. Kevin Fleming, clinical psychologist turned executive coach, was riding shotgun in the cab of a Ford pickup, traveling north on a dirt road in western Wyoming at a steady forty miles per hour. The day was warm, and the University of Notre Dame Ph.D. passed the time listening to the Joe Stampley CD in the player, muffled partly by the hum of air rushing through the open windows. The driver was a man named Tyke, an oil field worker whose job was to maintain forty pump-jack wells strung throughout this barren county of sagebrush and antelope.

Tyke was six and a half feet tall and wore large aviator glasses and a close-fitting blue T-shirt over a stomach that extended almost to the steering wheel. He was born in the South and raised on fried foods and sugary snacks. Occasionally Tyke would take a long draw from a soda bottle or reach into a chip bag, and the psychologist would pull out his notebook and scribble something. It had been going on like this for several days. The pumper (as Tyke called his job title) would drive hundreds of miles in a ten-hour shift, stopping periodically to fix broken tubing, grease a valve, or take a reading on one of his nodding donkey wells, and then would climb back in the cab, where he would eat or drink again, and the psychologist would record what he saw.

Occasionally the doc would ask a question. *What would get you to pass up a pizza place and order a salad? How many sodas do you drink in a day? Have you ever tried tofu? It's not so bad, you know. Do you know at what age you are estimated to die?*

Dr. Kevin Fleming was on a mission. For more than a year he'd been riding along with oil field workers such as Tyke. His goal was to help these men and women live longer, to reduce the incidence of heart disease and cancer that was killing so many in their profession. The oil company had hired him to influence behavior, but first he explained he needed to influence belief. And to do that, he had to get into the minds of a group of tough-as-nails pumpers and roughnecks. In the end, the company *was* able to influence the behavior of its workers and wellness improved. But it wasn't easy. Beliefs don't change overnight.

At the beginning of their diet or fitness programs, the changes they were choosing to make were forced. They didn't like eating healthy food or exercising. It was hard work. It didn't feel good. And the only reward was a sense of short-term accomplishment and maybe the fact that their friends and family patted them on the back or simply stopped pestering them about their habits. But as the physiological change in their bodies began to form, the reward system changed as well. More began to feel a boost in their self-esteem. Many actually started to feel good when they exercised. The healthy foods started to trigger reward systems in their bodies because they were receiving nutritional replenishment. And yes, some even developed a taste for tofu (and some didn't; after all, it *is* tofu).

Said Fleming, "The interesting aspect of weight loss that is relatable to workplace culture and belief is the moment when the person who lost the weight says, 'I get it now. It clicked and now it makes sense.' That's the point where the brain allows the new belief system to be right. And for most people, that is a transformational moment—their belief system changed."

That people would begin to believe in a new way of acting once they begin to experience intrinsic rewards is easy to understand. What's the tricky part, of course, is the front end of the process, the stage when nothing feels like it makes sense, even though the change is perfectly sensible—even proven by data. Fleming had some powerful insights about how to help people through this phase.

Since his time in the oil fields of Wyoming, the Cowboy Shrink (as Fleming is known) has become a thought-leader in corporate psychology and he founded the company Grey Matters International, which works with executive teams to help them drive success. Despite the Ph.D. hanging on his wall, Fleming was never your stereotypical couch therapist. Even when he was doing traditional counseling, he had a reputation for being aggressively blunt and uncomfortably inquisitive with his clients. He offered absolute truth and transparency.

True to form, the first words Fleming spoke to us when we met with him were a succinct, "What's this all about?" We explained that we had found that a culture where people *believe* is more profitable, and that we wanted to learn about the psychology of belief. That's when Fleming interrupted and said, "First, understand that our brains are wired to *feel* right, not necessarily *be* right," he said. "That's where you need to start."

Reinforcing what we've already written, he explained, "Our brain is wired to want to prove that our behaviors and feelings are justified and have reason. We all want to prove we're right. Managers want to prove they're right. Employees want to prove they're right. And when you combine all these people into one organization, you can end up with an egocentric system collision."

When we asked him to elaborate, he said, "Too often leaders state who they are and if people don't share their same beliefs, those employees quickly learn to do what I call a cost/benefit ratio dance—they minimize the dissonance they feel by showing up and doing the minimal amount necessary to seem like a team player."

How then can a leader align beliefs and build a culture?

"You have to understand the complexity of the brain," he explained. "For example, new employees enter your workplace with their own beliefs. If you immediately try to align their beliefs with those of the culture, the brain can switch into self-protective mode. Those employees might not hear the benefits of what you're saying, but they could make you think they do.

So the net effect of this self-protective dance is that they might superficially accept your leadership, rejecting it whenever it suits their purpose, claiming, 'I never really bought in.' Which actually is quite true! In fact, this is ninety-nine percent of the pain I work with."

As Fleming shared this with us, we realized it means that as leaders we must first allow people on our teams to feel like valuable individuals, respecting their views and opening up to their ideas and inputs, even while sharing a better way forward. It's a balancing act that requires some wisdom.

"Let's face it, early leaders didn't survive on the savanna by diplomacy," said Fleming. "Our brains as leaders are hardwired to survive, save face, and make us feel that we're right. But being right and being wise are very different things, with dramatically different outcomes."

And being wise means we learn when to act and when not to. Fleming says the best leaders regularly ask themselves two questions:

"What do I have to do right now to help my people do their best?"

and . . .

"What should I not do right now to help my people do their best?"

This may mean doing nothing except staying out of an employee's way. For instance, if a worker truly buys into your purpose and goals, managerial action may actually be detrimental to the employee's performance, engagement, or relationship with you, because it may lead them to believe that they're not trusted.

As for the nonbelievers: Fleming says many books will tell you the key to finding out what your people think is to ask them. "That's logical, until we consider the reality of that process.

Companies are structured in hierarchies. So when we ask people to tell us what they think—or believe—we must consider the fact that the brain is hardwired to protect us. *Employees won't speak the truth if they think that truth won't be heard or integrated.* And most managers won't truly listen to their employees' beliefs if they perceive those beliefs as opposing forces."

We learned this lesson early in our careers. In one of his first jobs out of college, Chester was working for a woman who acted as if she was infallible. Riding in a taxi to an appointment in Manhattan, the boss asked him, "Do you like your job?" It was a time of intense pressure in the organization, and the workplace was truly miserable, but the young Chester thought, *There's no way I'm giving an honest answer.* So he said, "Oh, I love my job." The boss's response? She swore at him, repeated the curse in case he missed it, and then went silent for the remainder of the cab ride.

As a newcomer to the corporate world, he had felt in a no-win situation. He knew he couldn't be candid with such a misanthropic boss, and yet when he tried to fake his way out of the situation she saw right through it. When they arrived at the appointment Chester called his wife and said, "Honey, get a For Sale sign on our lawn before I get home. I don't know where we are going or what job we are going to get, but we aren't going to stay here."

While meetings between leaders and employees are rarely that extreme, the vast majority go this way: Leaders ask for input from their teams. Teams tell the manager just enough of what they believe the manager wants to hear to protect their survival. After all, they know that if someone shares a view that is against the manager's or team's beliefs the chances are very good that it won't be embraced or that it will be given what Fleming calls pseudo-acceptance, a state of "not overtly rejecting something while maintaining wiggle room for self-benefit."

Obviously this is not a sustainable way to operate, and leaders ask Fleming how to fix it. "They ask how to get the truth out of their employees. Notice how they've already blamed the employee. And that's the problem."

He said, "The key is not to get rid of the squeaky wheels. Instead, leaders should consider why the wheels are squeaking. It's possible that all the other wheels are actually the problem and the squeaky wheels are simply communicating the problem."

If a leader truly wants to read the bubbles over their team's heads, the simple solution is this: "Don't crap on the data or the feedback," he said. "And not only that—actively seek evidence that disconfirms what you believe, even reward it when you hear it."

One more personal story about how we've experienced this challenge firsthand. Once, when Adrian was still a naïve corporate communications leader, he approached his company president and earnestly told him morale was on the decline in the firm. "I've been listening to employees grumble in the break room and on the shop floor. They even complain to each other over the stalls in the men's room. The situation is, well, disquieting." The president smiled kindly, as if Adrian were a misguided kindergartener, and explained, "If morale were so"—he paused before repeating the near-euphemism—"*disquieting*, well then surely my executive team would have told me."

Adrian left the president's office bewildered. He knew of course that the man's leadership team wasn't about to admit employee engagement was in the dumps. It would have been an admission that these men and women were failing in their roles. It took months before he was able to start persuading the company's president that employees were fed up.

Fleming argued that the vital first step in bringing about transformations of belief in one's employees is awakening within ourselves, as managers, the recognition that the real truth of any belief is actually not as black and white as we thought.

"The leader who holds most dearly to the unbreakable nature of their belief is the one I am most worried about, for that pride gets projected in the name of righteousness. Most problems around promoting shared belief in organizations come from this subtle misguidedness—where we attempt to change others' beliefs while holding on to the supremacy of our own."

*   *   *

After listening to Fleming, you might ask yourself if trying to change your people's beliefs is really worth the effort or even possible. *If I have to admit that my own beliefs might be wrong, will I really get enough of a payoff?* To answer, let us turn next to the astonishing power positive belief can deliver.

≈ ALL IN ≈

THE CHA-CHA DANCER WHO BELIEVED HE COULD FIGHT

In the spring of 1959, the Chinese mafia allegedly issued a contract on the life of an eighteen-year-old ballroom dancer named Bruce Lee. The sinewy Hong Kong cha-cha champion and high school boxing titleholder had a penchant for getting into street fights on the weekends, something he actually enjoyed and was quite good at. And while you might argue the merits of Lee's pastime, there's no doubt his selection of opponents lacked sound judgment. One of the young men he'd beaten was supposedly the son of a feared Hong Kong triad family, and the mob wanted revenge. Lee was nonchalant, continuing to stroll the streets of his hometown with a swagger, so his father made a decision for him. He packed his son's duffel bag and put him on the next ocean liner to the United States.

Bruce Lee arrived in San Francisco with a hundred dollars in his pocket and a truly maverick notion: that fighting prowess wasn't about size or strength, but about an iron-willed belief that you could win every single contest. Conventional wisdom at the time dictated that a taller, heavier, stronger man would win ninety-nine out of a hundred brawls against a smaller opponent. Lee scoffed at the notion and started competing in martial arts matches against much larger men—all to bring attention to the idea that bigger wasn't necessarily better. He described his opponents as throwing "wall-shaker" punches that if landed could have killed him, and yet the five-foot-eight-inch Lee systematically took apart all comers, explaining, "The important thing for any fighter is to beat him mentally and emotionally, to knock down his spirit and make him believe he can be stopped."

In one exhibition, Lee faced a formidable Japanese martial arts champion. The Japanese black belt arrived at the fight in full *gi* (uniform) and ran through an impressive *kata*—an intricate choreography of spin kicks, blocks, and power punches. Lee watched all of this in his street clothes, leaning casually against a pile of blocking pads in the corner until the big Japanese champion had finished his warm-up. Finally Lee approached the mat, slipped off his tennis shoes, bowed, and then with blinding speed hit the fellow fifteen times, kicked him once, and casually walked off while organizers scrambled to call an ambulance for the unconscious opponent. The clock was stopped. The entire fight had lasted eleven seconds.

Word spread. After all, this was not normal. Most fights, especially with men the size of Lee, were drawn-out affairs, with one man eventually wearing down the other. Smaller martial artists, or lightweight boxers for that matter, just didn't have the strength to deliver knockout power so early in a fight. Why was this man so different? Because Bruce Lee believed his body could accomplish any task placed before it. "A powerful athlete is not a strong athlete, but one who can exert his strength quickly," he explained. "A smaller man who can swing faster may hit as hard or as far as the heavier man who swings slowly."

With such views, Lee quickly gained great popularity, appearing in television shows and movies in the sixties and seventies. He even became a fixture on TV's *The Green Hornet*. It is safe to say that this one man's extraordinary prowess led to the proliferation and popularization of martial arts in the Western world. He showed us that even an average person could break a brick with his hand, bust through a wall, or send flying a hefty opponent with just a one-inch punch (as Lee demonstrated to amazed audiences). Suddenly moms and dads were signing their children up for kung fu lessons, so they could stand up to bullies and at least break a few bones if challenged in a dark alley.

Bruce Lee showed what the human body is capable of on a martial arts mat, just as Michael Jordan did on a basketball court, Muhammad Ali did in the ring, Pelé did on a soccer pitch, Steffi Graf did on a tennis court, and Michael Phelps did in the water.

In 1996, Deborah Phelps had just realized her son Michael had a gift. In a swimming pool he was fast, very fast. And yet Michael had a racing habit that his mother explained thus: "Michael is a 'comeback' swimmer. In most cases he is behind in his races. Then at the last moment, with a burst of energy and an iron-willed belief he will win, he comes from behind to win the race. He believes that he can win every race as long as he is in the pool. He never gives up on his belief that he can win."

Now, it would be ludicrous to deny the obvious: Michael Phelps has a near-ideal body for his sport. Unlike like the diminutive Bruce Lee, who never fit his role, Phelps looks the part. He's six foot four but swims even taller. If you give him an appraising glance you'll notice that Phelps has an usually long torso in relation to his legs, which gives him less drag. He also has the wingspan of a man at least six feet seven inches tall, a textbook set of muscles, long feet, and hands the size of dinner plates—all of which help propel him through the water like a torpedo. Add in the fact that Phelps is smart enough to understand the mechanics of his sport (he's learned when to glide and when to take a half stroke at the end of a race, for instance) and his barbarous practice regime, and you have the makings of a champion.

It's an impressive list of qualities. But it doesn't explain his success. You see, it's also the list that describes most of the world's elite swimmers—hundreds and hundreds of tall, fit, smart athletes who could all swim circles around the rest of us.

Perhaps, then, it's Phelps's competitive nature that sets him apart? That assumption would be wrong, says Eddie Reese, the U.S. men's swim team coach at the 2004 and 2008 Olympics. He describes his team this way: "Eighty percent of swimmers like to win, 20 percent hate to lose, and 95 percent of the Olympic team comes from the hate-to-lose group."

So Phelps is not uniquely built; most swimmers are lanky and strong. And he's not uniquely competitive; just about everyone who splashes into an Olympic pool will move heaven and earth to avoid coming in second.

So to understand the difference, let's back up and understand his story. Phelps started swimming competitively when he was just seven. Admittedly he was hardly a world-class talent at the time. In fact, five good but not great years later, Phelps's coach Bob Bowman called a meeting with Mom, Dad, and athlete, sticking the little swimmer in the middle with nowhere to run or hide. Bowman said it was time to get serious. He had to step it up, to do what he was told, or he wouldn't swim anymore—at least not at Bowman's club. Phelps could be something special, but only if he believed in himself enough to stop crying, complaining, and horsing around.

The swimmer listened. Phelps not only stepped up his game, but he qualified for the 2000 Olympics, where he came in fifth in the 200-meter butterfly. An impressive feat for anyone, but Phelps was only fifteen years old.

It was a promising start, but chances are Michael Phelps would be little more than another good Olympic swimmer if he hadn't had another major change in his mind-set leading up to the Athens Olympics. Phelps developed a belief that he could not only win an Olympic gold medal one day but win enough gold medals in the same games to beat Mark Spitz's miraculous 1972 record of seven golds.

And it was his manager who gave him the notion and the confidence.

Bob Bowman, who had pushed the twelve-year-old Phelps to focus and believe he could be great, now refined Phelps's natural drive and dedication to get him to consider chasing this much bigger dream. Phelps said of his coach, "He has, without question, helped me believe that anything is possible. Two seconds faster than the world record? Doesn't matter. Three seconds? Doesn't matter. You can swim as fast as you want."

In the 2003 world championships in Barcelona, Phelps—who

had just turned eighteen—won an astounding four gold medals and broke five world records. And yet as word spread of Phelps's dream of taking home a record amount of gold at the 2004 Olympics, few people outside of his inner circle felt it was a possibility. Newspapers quoted the former head coach of Australia's swim team as saying that Phelps had yet to prove himself on the global stage with real pressure. The number one swimmer in the world at the time, Ian Thorpe, had to admit that breaking Spitz's record was "unattainable for me and unattainable for anyone."

The next year in Athens Phelps took home six Olympic gold medals. And still he and Bowman knew they could do better. Oddly enough, the other person to readily agree was fifty-eight-year-old Mark Spitz himself, the holder of the record with seven gold medals in one games. The former champion showed up at training camp near the end of the 2008 trials to tell anyone who would listen that Phelps was going to win eight in Beijing. "He's going to do it. Records are made to be broken. I swam a long time ago, and it's okay, it's okay."

Spitz was indeed prophetic. In Beijing, Phelps was breaking world records not by fractions but by full seconds and more, not just because his body or talent was superior. As Phelps explained, "I believe in myself."

"With belief, with confidence and trust in yourself and those around you, there are no limits," he concluded, weighed down at the time with the impressive collection of gold around his neck.

It's hard to argue with a man sporting that much precious metal. And yet if the stories of a swimmer and a martial artist seem a far cry from your reality, consider instead the example of Starbucks CEO Howard Schultz, who in 2008 took back his struggling chain of coffeehouses and put it back on the road to belief. Kicking off this rebirth of perception with an honest assessment of the company's current situation, Schultz sent an e-mail to all employees telling them that Starbucks was losing the "romance and theatre" so core to its defining DNA. But he then expressed a sincere belief that his team had the talent to rally.

When we met Schultz in New York in 2011, in recalling the turning point he said, "I believed that Starbucks had an enormous potential to return to greatness, that the company had yet to be as good as it was going to be. I believed in the power of the brand, in our founding mission, and most of all, in our people.

"I really did believe."

But this CEO knew he needed to get his people to believe too, and that meant a return to the basics. Part of that process was to shut down every one of the 7,100 locations on a Tuesday afternoon, costing the company $6 million in revenue, to teach the 135,000 baristas how to pour a perfect shot of espresso. Schultz said, "We had lost the essence of what we set out to do forty years ago, inspire the human spirit. I realize this is a lofty mission for a cup of coffee, but this is what merchants do. We take the ordinary—a shoe, a knife—and give it new life, believing that what we create has the potential to touch others' lives . . . Without great coffee, we have no reason to exist."

The result? Starbucks saw a 400 percent increase in its share price from 2008 to 2011, as not only employees but shareholders have learned to believe again.

So, yes, making a concerted effort to learn how to get your people to believe is definitely worth the work. And what we will show—what is so central to our message—is that doing so doesn't have to be a matter of bringing people around one by one. As a culture of belief grows past the influence of one leader, it can still sweep people up in itself and begin to take on a life of its own.

≈ ALL IN ≈

CULTURE IS CONTAGIOUS

Many managers are loath to admit it—depending on their work group's level of engagement, enablement, and energy on the job—but the influence of our work culture is pervasive. Cultures are a little like viruses. People can't help but be infected by the place where they spend eight, nine, or ten hours a day. When someone drops into a new culture, they absorb its influence in many ways. And likewise one infected person can cause a shift in an entire culture—for good or bad.

If our studies and others have illustrated the substantial positive impact an effective corporate culture can have on an organization's performance, employee engagement, and customer service, then why do so many of us still not take it seriously?

It certainly was not something our friend Pat considered when he accepted a job as an insurance underwriter at a mid-sized agency on the East Coast. He wasn't necessarily focused on finding a great cultural fit. He said he wanted to work for a fair boss who appreciated his skill set. Don't we all. Pat also wanted a place where there might be opportunities to grow, and he wanted the security of a steady paycheck at a stable company.

Our friend showed up for work and was pleasantly surprised. The atmosphere wasn't like other companies he'd worked for. Instead of the stiff, top-down, command-and-control atmosphere he was accustomed to in the insurance game, the employees at his new company were involved in decision-making, they were garrulous, and they enjoyed a healthy dose of levity in the workplace.

Soon Pat felt comfortable and valued, and he felt a kinship with his coworkers and their boss. He lunched daily with the gang at one of the fine local eateries. He took breaks every day at 9:45 and 2:45 to grab a soda and a doughnut with his manager and new buddies. And a few times a week he went out after work for beers with the gang.

Sounds like a great fit, right? Indeed, the culture was already having an impact on Pat. Within three months he was more absorbed in his work than he'd ever been . . . and he'd gained twenty-one pounds. Seriously.

We should come clean and admit that when Pat told us this we couldn't help but shake our heads and chuckle. After all, this isn't the impact anyone assumes is a result of culture, but it demonstrates a significant point—it may take a long time for a manager to influence a person, but once a collective culture is established it can change people in a hurry. Cultures can influence perspectives, expectations, belief systems, and even the biology of their members.

A study by Harvard researchers and others showed the number of obese friends a person has can increase the chance that that person will become obese, suggesting that weight gain spreads through social networks. "We find that having four obese friends doubled people's chance of becoming obese compared with people with no obese friends," said Alison Hill, the study's lead author and a Harvard University researcher.

In its most basic form, that research reveals the impact a small group of people can have on those around them and their behaviors. Now imagine the cumulative impact that a group of passionate, committed people at your company can have on a whole department, and scaling up, on the organization as a whole.

As we go forward in this book, we are going to build on the ideas from social psychology that we've explored here and introduce the key findings that every manager can use to create a culture of belief and reap the rewards of its self-reinforcing positivity. First we'll take a closer look at the three key ways employees must feel in order for you to have a true culture of belief: engaged, enabled, and energized. And then we'll dive into the seven steps that are so crucial in bringing this about. Along the way we'll learn how these ideas helped a chain of rock and roll restaurants flourish through one of the worst recessions in history, how they focused a complex financial services company on improving customer service in the midst of the world's banking meltdown, and how they might have kept a bankrupt automaker from disaster.

What lies ahead in these pages is a journey toward helping others believe in you and with you. We begin at the end, with a team that is living these principles.

3

E + E + E

The Competitive Advantage
of the New Economy

On a thundery morning in Fort Lauderdale, only a few miles from where U2 played a few nights before, a crowded indoor atrium begins to take on the feel of a rock concert. Businesspeople are hanging over six floors of balconies looking down at a collection of dancers on the main floor. Then, at the urging of the lead performer, just about everyone in the building suddenly starts moving to the pulsing strains of a recording by Lady Gaga, throwing their fists in the air and shouting, "Just dance!"

When the music ends the crowd roars. The lead dancer, a middle-aged woman in a business suit, waves up at the gathering. Hundreds of people are laughing and cheering another performance by Doria Camaraza and her leadership team.

Doria who?

This mild-mannered, bespectacled woman is the senior vice president and general manager of this American Express World Service Center, located in two nondescript buildings in an industrial park in southern Florida. This is a 3,000-person call center, and the work is not easy. Customers call when they need help with a lost card or want to make an address change. Others want to dispute charges or can't find their bill. And some are upset; perhaps they don't qualify for a credit increase. Yet despite the often demanding atmosphere, Camaraza and her fellow senior managers have found a way to get just about all of these people to believe in what they are trying to accomplish. In fact, we might argue that she and her team are the best bunch of leaders of believers you've never heard of—bad dancing and all.

Here's some proof: Around the United States, employee turnover in call centers averages about 50 percent annually. That means if you answer phones for a living, about half your coworkers will leave before another year passes. Not here. Turnover in Fort Lauderdale is in the single digits annually. Let us pause for a moment to let that sink in: Turnover is less than one-fifth the national average.

But there's more: Productivity measures are tops in the call center industry.

Six years ago, when Camaraza took over, the call center was good. Today it's great—helping American Express earn an unprecedented five consecutive years of J. D. Power & Associates awards for highest customer satisfaction among credit card companies. Very impressive.

But boogying in front of your employees? This is, after all, American Express—one of the world's most prestigious business brands, and you might argue one of the most serious. Not here, says Camaraza. She calls this American Express facility a "community of caring," and the leadership team dances every month in the atrium to get attention before the real business of this meeting, called "Tribute"—spotlighting employees who've gone above and beyond and those who are celebrating long-tenure service awards. As soon as the music ends, Camaraza retires to what she calls her "Oprah chairs," two beige loungers, where she interviews a series of employees who are being spotlighted publicly for living the American Express values.

She begins with an employee from platinum-card member services who helped a stranded customer find a hotel room—despite the fact that the customer had left home without his card. "Sam spent an hour and a half on the phone until he found a hotel that would let this card member check in without his card," she explains. "That's living our Blue Box value of customer commitment. Sam has made a real difference in that customer's life." The large crowd heartily applauds the fellow's accountability as Camaraza presents him with an award from RewardBlue—American Express' recognition system where any employee can recognize any other employee in forty-five countries.

After welcoming another eight people to the spotlight in the Oprah chairs, and getting misty-eyed on a few occasions as she describes someone's dedication, Camaraza steps aside and on cue a randomly selected employee from each of the facility's large business units runs out. The blaring music returns and the five play a game of Minute to Win It, blowing up balloons and then using the captured air to try to push fifteen cups off their respective tables. The crowd begins howling in encouragement for their floors' representatives and laughing hysterically at some of the attempts. When a slight, spunky woman from the credit group wins, employees from the fourth floor go bananas in celebration.

"Loosening up like this was especially important when we were going through the financial crisis," Camaraza says. "Our people were working so hard. Every call that came in seemed to be challenging: Someone had lost their job and wasn't making their payments. We had to help folks relieve the stress of a very tough environment."

But surely some people don't approve of such shenanigans. True, though such cranky attitudes don't last long in Fort Lauderdale. "I don't want to surround myself with people who are dragging themselves to work. We don't need any grumpy poopoo heads," Camaraza said. "That's a technical term," she added with a chuckle, and we couldn't help but laugh with her.

All this cheerfulness and productivity in today's financial services industry is rare and is derived in part from leadership's unique efforts to affect employees' physical and emotional well-being—something that has paid off for them handsomely. For instance, Camaraza walked us through their brand-new Healthy Living Center, a workout facility with fitness classes and weights. Trainers are on staff, as is a nurse. And then she gave us a tour of the Kids Zone, a backup child-care facility. As we entered, "Who Let the Dogs Out?" was blaring from a television as a dozen excited eight-year-olds bounced in front of a video dance game as part of an exercise break.

CEO Ken Chenault and executive vice president of world service Jim Bush gave Camaraza the go-ahead to pilot the facility in Fort Lauderdale. "We have about ninety births here every year and eleven hundred dependent children under the age of twelve," Camaraza explained. "It was a significant multimillion-dollar investment that paid back in about fifteen months. It's a huge driver in reducing absenteeism, and we can look at the attrition of people who are registered for child care and the rest of the employee population and there is no comparison."

Employees are eligible for up to twenty days of backup child care in the facility and three weeks of summer camp for their kids. And employees' newborns can spend up to eight weeks in the Kids Zone. "A woman who has no children said to me today that it makes [her] really proud to work for this company. We get a ripple effect that is really powerful," Camaraza said.

Reflecting on the positive culture at the facility, Lisa Telfer, director of business planning, told us, "You might ask why would anyone want to settle down for sixteen years in one place, but when you talk with people here you get it. You are treated well, there's an amazing level of care and concern. And when employees are happy, that translates to customers." Charles Johnson, the center's HR relationship leader, said, "This is not a utopia. But if you have to work, it doesn't get much better than this."

In the six years this leadership team has run this facility, it has certainly been a wildly productive environment but also a hopeful and happy place. And while each of the leaders admits they are not perfect as managers, these executives have about three thousand followers who love working here—three thousand people who truly believe in the mission and values they're asked to follow through on.

If all this esprit de corps seems a bit overwhelming to achieve in your workplace—in your lifetime—realize that you wouldn't be

the first manager we've worked with to push back about under-
taking a culture shift with this level of dedication. *It wouldn't
work here,* you might think. That's okay. Not every manager has
to go to these lengths to inject life into their culture. But there are
lessons for us all to learn in Fort Lauderdale. For instance, Doria
Camaraza has come to understand that being a manager doesn't
mean knowing products and services, it means knowing your
people. "I don't have much business being in this role. I don't
have the right technical background. But the role of a manager
isn't about being technically proficient. It's about people."

Another lesson? The culture starts at the top, said Telfer.
"Everyone has a Doria story; there are three thousand stories.
People don't know how she remembers so much about them, but
she literally works at making people feel welcomed and wonderful. Despite her insane body of responsibilities, she's in touch
with her people. Not to mention she goes to Zumba and cardio
kickboxing classes with employees here on the campus. Who
does *that*?"

This culture is very strong, very positive, and most important,
is leading to very real results for a very large and complex organization. And Camaraza and her leadership team have kept up
this kind of productivity and energy through the worst financial meltdown in our lifetime. How do they engender that kind
of loyalty and commitment? This American Express call center
is a case study in developing a culture of belief, with managers
who are benefiting from E + E + E in action. They have achieved
world-class levels of efficiency, profitability, and customer satisfaction because their employees are:

Engaged. They understand how their work benefits the larger
organization and have a clear understanding of how they are
responsible and accountable for real results. And they can see
the value of their contributions to the company's larger mission.

Enabled. The company supports employees with the right tools
and training, and leaders spend 75 percent of their time coach-

ing and walking the floor to ensure that workers can navigate the demands of their jobs.

Energized. Leaders at this facility maintain feelings of well-being and high levels of energy through daily productivity contests, helping employees balance work and home life, and recognizing individual contributions. In fact, at American Express, nearly 20,000 times a month employees are praised for effort or rewarded for results via the RewardBlue system (we'll go into this in more detail in chapter 9).

≈ ALL IN ≈

REMEMBER, ENGAGEMENT IS NOT ENOUGH

The notion that an employee needs to be engaged, enabled, or energized is certainly not groundbreaking. But the problem is that they've generally been considered separately. Instead, think for a moment about these three traits visually, as shaded circles in a Venn diagram; when the three traits overlap, their three colors combine to form a darker, richer tone. Any one without the other two is good but not sufficient for truly exceptional results.

A hamster on a treadmill is energized, for example, but it doesn't really accomplish much by spinning its wheel. It isn't enabled to take the wheel out for a spin in the woods. Likewise, an eager new military cadet may be engaged. He may care about the corps and be eager to serve his country, but without training and the right support, he's unlikely to be of much use to his comrades. A teenager can be given all of the enabling freedom in the world, but if she isn't absorbed in an interesting challenge, she will likely be bored rather than energized and won't accomplish much. Each element of E + E + E can be held hostage by an imbalance in the other two.

The flip side is that each of the three, when present, builds on the others, or you could say they combine as in a chemical reaction, becoming combustible.

As we have traveled around the world, we have found

that most organizations regularly assess where they stand on employee engagement, using attitude surveys or pulse surveys. But to address real needs and move forward, they must also assess how enabled and energized their people feel. Determining the degree of E + E + E on a corporate level typically involves quantitative surveys, focus groups, and benchmarking against organizations in similar industries. And yet to understand the specific dynamics of their particular team, managers can conduct a simple analysis of their own. The key is that you must be able to interpret conversations and jump-start honest face-to-face dialogue in order to make ongoing assessments through less structured, more intuitive means.

Below we provide three questions to help you start to determine if any of your team members are disengaged, dis-enabled, or un-energized. As you read the questions, take a moment to think about your team:

- ❑ Do you have employees who care about the organization but are burned out?
- ❑ Do you have people who are energized to do big things but feel stifled and not able to run?
- ❑ Do you have employees who care but aren't always focused on the right behaviors?

Did anyone come to mind? You most likely came up with clear images of people on your team or perhaps those in other areas of the company who match those descriptions. Does that mean they're "problem children" you should give up on? Not at all. But in most cases, by thinking about which element of E + E + E might be an issue for your employees, you can begin to help them make needed corrections. For instance, Julie is a real go-getter with lots of ideas and energy, but she's spending so much time on what's supposed to be a small assignment—updating your social media sites—that her day job of setting up new customers is suffering. Jared has been one of your most productive people for several years. He'd walk in front of a train for you or the company, which is probably why he never says no to new assignments. The pressure is sapping his drive, he's short-tempered and overwhelmed, and he mentioned last week that his new girlfriend has just about had it with all the long hours. No matter how much you are paying him, it's not enough. As you can see, it's fruitless for an employee to feel engaged without feeling he or she is energized to sustain momentum or enabled to succeed on the team's real priorities. Each driver is unable to sustain your success long-term without the other accompanying elements.

Iva Ros, a researcher at Towers Watson, says, "It was fascinating to learn that engagement is just the first rung in the ladder; cultures must adapt and enable their people, they must deliver and energize. It's comforting in a way that there is a pathway for companies."

To help you assess the degree to which your own people are engaged, enabled, and energized, and to appreciate the powerful role each can play in boosting your results, we now take a deeper dive. As we do, consider the impact each element of E + E + E has, or could have, on your team, department, or organization. Think about your strengths and weaknesses, and especially your opportunities for improvement.

Engaged

Engagement is typically defined as a quality of employees who are willing to give discretionary effort, who care about the mission and values of the organization, and who show a willingness to recommend the company's products and services.

According to Towers Watson's 2010 Global Workforce Study—which includes representative national samples of full-time employees from twenty-two countries in every region of the globe—62 percent of employees are at least somewhat engaged at work; that's less than two-thirds. But the numbers get more dire: Only 21 percent of employees, or one in five, are fully engaged, giving their all to their workplaces, and an even a thinner slice (16 percent) have high levels of E + E + E. This of course leaves 38 percent of the typical workforce who can be labeled as somewhat or fully disengaged.

Researchers at Towers Watson tell us that when they survey a workplace, they can usually place individual employees at some point on this engagement continuum:

Disengaged. People who are divorced emotionally from the company and its values. In some cases, these people actively work against your goals or even attempt to sabotage your culture. They are a distinct threat to your brand, and they are toxic to those around them.

Disenfranchised. These individuals have been soured by something about their work experience. They may not purposely attempt to sabotage your organization, but their performance is marginal and their energy is often actively focused on seeking other employment.

Enrolled. People who are somewhat committed to the company or team and are giving a reasonable effort at work. However, they are open to other job offers and may view their employment as "temporary."

Engaged. These are team members who are committed to the company and its values. They'll give extra effort for customers, colleagues, and leadership. In short, they care.

Exponentially engaged. This new research shows employees who are engaged, enabled, and energized provide an organization with a much greater lift of performance. These employees with high E + E + E levels are not only highly committed to the company and its values in the present, but they are enabled to actively look for areas where they can add value to the organization in the future, and they have the energy to keep going and going. They not only focus on making the workplace and their work great today but also see how extra effort, great work, and passion can build additional opportunities—sharing ideas for innovation, seeking new and deeper relationships with clients, and streamlining processes to accelerate performance. These people are the hope of your organization; however, there is a caveat: They're supercharged not only because of who they are (intrinsically) but more important because of how they're treated (extrinsic motivation). They feel as if they have the support necessary to succeed, the opportunity to follow their personal dreams and aspirations, and the energy to sustain accelerated performance over time. We'll add to these ideas in the coming sections.

For now, let's just consider the idea of "engagement" by itself. The Towers Watson data shows that financial results in organizations with high employee engagement are 44 percent higher than in those with low engagement. The research further shows that cultures in which employees are engaged have a key set of characteristics. The mission and values of the company are clear, as are the standards and expectations for every employee. Also leaders work to make sure that employees understand the alignment of their work and actions to the larger company purpose, vision, and goals. Employees tend to be fitted well to their jobs. In addition, employees feel a sense of possibility and believe that they will grow while working at the company, if not through promotions then by achieving their personal goals and reaching for higher levels of competency and impact.

To understand this idea, we take you with us to the Dallas/Fort Worth airport to meet Carlos Aguilera, district manager of the Avis Budget Group location there. He has two hundred employees working three shifts a day, seven days a week, 365 days a year. On a typical Monday, their busiest day, they'll rent more than 2,400 vehicles. Aguilera told us he believes engagement should begin before day one—as early as the interview with a prospective new hire. "We'll talk about Avis Budget core values, what we are looking for. And I use myself as an example. I started out cleaning cars as a service agent. I explain how they can grow."

Those new employees will typically start on the weekend or

night shift. "That's our area of opportunity," Aguilera said. "If you can help those new associates engage on those late shifts, answer their questions, we will improve service." So Aguilera shows up at all sorts of odd hours. "They need to know I'm worrying about them, I'm not just a boss who works nine to five and then goes home."

And since engagement is influenced by a person's opportunities for development, this is one boss who devotes a lot of time to mentoring—consciously spending the most time with those who want to move up in the organization.

Aguilera has an intensity and love for his work and for his people that is infectious. As he describes his daily activities to us, it's as if he's describing a great passion in life—with the rich detail some would use to recall a championship game they played in high school or even an important family outing. And sensibly, at every point during the day, this manager is thinking, *How can I get my people to be just as passionate as I am?*

Heaven knows how much value is squandered by leaders who do not spend time engaging their people—those who don't recognize their dependence on their subordinates. And yet the rewards are huge when you stop trying to control and strive instead to engage people as part of a growing, thriving organization.

Enabled

For employees to be enabled, an organization must provide the right tools and equipment, but also clear daily direction from leadership, flexibility in how the job gets done, and help in meeting work obstacles and challenges. Enablement should not be confused with empowerment, a time-tested but much narrower idea. Yes, enabled employees certainly are empowered—allowed to make decisions in autonomous ways—but they also perform at a high level because they have the information needed to get past obstacles, well-defined processes, the right supplies, and equipment that works. The closest synonym for "enablement" is not "empowerment" but "support."

Towers Watson found net profit margins were 65 percent higher in companies reporting high levels of engagement *and* enablement, versus those firms with high engagement and low enablement—a powerful finding that suggests there may still be a significant performance boost hanging out there even if your engagement scores are above average.

In cultures where employees feel enabled, leaders hold themselves accountable for communicating the current state of affairs from a performance standpoint instead of leaving employees to wonder and guess what's going on. While engagement is about providing a link to the company's mission, enablement is first about providing concreteness about performance—how we are doing at a company, team, and individual level—with gains and declines openly tracked. It means employee performance is regularly evaluated; feedback from customers and employees—good and bad—is shared freely; and deadlines, revenue, timelines, and other metrics are honestly posted for all to see.

In addition, a good portion of an enabling leader's time is spent helping his or her people steer their way through choppy waters—not solving employee problems per se, but providing the communication employees need to make wise decisions in a changing environment, as well as offering the tools, resources, and clear expectations to help employees move forward successfully.

Let us explain one aspect of enablement with a quick story. We spent an hour in a high-tech firm in Manhattan one autumn day chatting amiably with a group of programmers. They were a genuinely motivated team and walked us through their projects with a passion that was refreshing. Then, in passing, they mentioned they'd been waiting for weeks to get six overhead fluorescent lights replaced. Silly problem, right? Then why did they bring it up to us? Because the whole place was dingy and gray and they felt as if they weren't getting the support they needed to do their jobs.

How could their manager help them? *How about some light!* Ever wondered something similar, like *Can I get a computer that*

works? Or *How about a phone that gets more than one bar?*
This is support at its most basic level, but having the right tools
and equipment is a key part of feeling enabled.

And yet even more important is a sense of *openness.* Carlos
Aguilera of the Avis Budget Group's Dallas/Fort Worth airport
location admits that in past years, his preshift meetings were
only for managers. Today he's learned that in order to help all
his people deal with the changing market, he needs to involve
employees. "In our meetings we talk about new developments
very openly. We ask our employees, 'What can we do better?
What can we do differently?' They help us think out of the box.
For instance, we just got these new Camaros. An employee said,
'Let's take a picture of them and have it in a digital frame on the
counter.' The employees think it will work, so we are going to
try it."

Consider for a moment that example, of new Camaros arriv-
ing at the location. It's a change in inventory that might cause
consternation in some rental car offices. The company has
invested several hundred thousand dollars in these new cars and
they aren't doing much good baking under the Texas sun. Your
typical business traveler isn't allowed to rent high-end vehicles
and most pleasure travelers booking online will opt for cheaper
cars. It's one of those little changes work groups are asked to deal
with every day. Aguilera meets it head-on by clarifying expectations and allowing for flexibility in the solution by enrolling his
people in a discussion.

This is enabling, supportive behavior at its most basic, and it's
a small part of a process Aguilera has used to allow employees
throughout this location to feel more involved in the business.
Staff at all levels are now able to forecast vehicle demand, check
equipment and supplies, and think up creative ways to market
and sell. It's allowed them to fill in for a manager who's on vacation or simply be more independent in their work.

"Instead of answering questions, we ask employees what
they would do. It's created a lot less interruptions. I told one

employee whose son plays soccer, 'Could your son make that three-hundred-and-sixty-degree Maradona move on the first try? Sometimes he tripped over the ball, right? You will make some mistakes, but you can do it. Keep trying.'"

Aguilera instinctively knows the importance of supporting and involving his people. Most of us are well aware that rather than enabling employees to take part in solving problems this way, many cultures stifle their people. How about the anonymous letter sent to the blog site BGR.com in the summer of 2011? The unnamed "high-level employee" at Research in Motion (you know them as the makers of BlackBerry) began his public letter to senior managers with, "I have lost confidence."

Research in Motion brass has questioned the validity of the missive, but BGR assured readers they verified the person's identity. (You can find a link to the letter on our website at TheCultureWorks.com.) It's a wonderfully crafted letter that represents the feelings of many in the corporate world and correlates directly with the findings of the research data in this book. The employee suggested that the main way to respond to the increasingly competitive mobile-device market was to democratize. "Interact with your employees—please. Reach out to all employees asking them how we can make RIM better. Encourage input from ground-level teams—without repercussions—to seek out honest feedback and really absorb it."

The writer's comments might ring true to those of us who, at some point in our careers, have worked at a place where leaders thought they had all the answers but clammed up during challenging times and didn't have the vision or provide the tools needed to meet challenges.

Too many of our employees have more to give, but they feel as if they are working in an environment where their management doesn't give them the information they need to succeed. If employees feel as if managers are enabling them to thrive on their own, they are more likely to view the entire company through a happier lens.

Energized

No matter how enabled or engaged workers are, pressures mount, relationships are tested, and well-being is jeopardized. To sustain their best work, employees need to feel part of an environment that keeps energy at a high level. Just as you need to avoid burnout as a leader, to build a high-performance culture you must in turn care about your employees' physical, emotional, and social well-being. That idea of "well-being" might be the most synonymous with the concept of being energized.

In the shelves and shelves of books on leadership, energy has received scant attention. We all know employees need it, but no one seems to know how to generate it. And yet consider what the lack of attention to this issue might cost you in employee stress, turnover, and lack of attention to customer needs. Another study by Towers Watson examined two divisions of a large multinational company, each with almost identical employee engagement scores. In the first division employees had favorable feelings of well-being and energy; in the other they had unfavorable feelings. The division with high energized scores improved its engagement score over a year by four percentage points, while engagement in the division with low well-being and energy declined by an alarming ten points. In short, being energized sustained the engagement necessary to maintain business performance during difficult times.

People in cultures where employees are energized know their leaders care about their well-being and that the company supports them inside and outside of work—even allowing them to maintain a positive work-life balance. There are also strong correlations between employees being energized and how regularly appreciated they feel. And, interestingly, we found the feeling of being energized is linked to the level of trust employees have in their managers. After all, few things sap energy faster than working for a manager who can't be trusted, one who doesn't uphold the core principles of the organization. And to follow that chain, a key driver of trust is open communication, which we also saw is a key aspect of enablement—because it is energizing and enabling to be included, to be on the "inside." Great cultures share information daily, even hourly.

So in addition to the more obvious ways of attending to the energy needs of employees, leaders must understand the uplifting effect on their people of open communication, keeping promises, recognizing great work, and work-life balance. All of this helps keep the best people in the culture.

For a few ideas, let's return for the last time to Carlos Aguilera's offices at Avis Budget in Dallas/Fort Worth. It's early, a preshift meeting. These gatherings of managers and employees never run more than twenty minutes and kick off with a bit of good-natured ribbing and even a smattering of talk about last night's episode of *Dancing with the Stars*. Aguilera pauses at one point when he feels the group is lagging and asks, "Okay, who saw someone doing something great yesterday?" A shift manager quickly brings up Genieva, who noticed one of her customers was wearing a knee brace. Genieva, without being asked, called an attendant and asked if the customer's car could be brought up to the front. The story takes about thirty seconds to tell, and the energy has returned to the meeting. Aguilera presents Genieva with an on-the-spot award. "And we make sure her accomplishment is posted on the bulletin board," he said to us later.

That may have been so quick you might have missed what just happened there. It's actually a super example; take a second to reread that last paragraph. Don't focus on the boss's recognition but on Genieva's actions that warranted the well-deserved praise. They speak volumes about how genuine this culture is. Here's a busy employee working the counter who notices a person wearing a knee brace. She didn't have to check a rulebook; she just acted. She called around back and asked an attendant to bring around a car. How great is that? Sure, it might seem like a trivial thing, but it's the kind of behavior that is happening every hour of every day because the culture works.

Let's continue with Aguilera for a little longer. As soon as he breaks the meeting, he taps one of the rental sales agents on the shoulder and they take a walk to the service center in the back lot, where rows and rows of cars are waiting to be vacuumed and washed. As they walk they chat about how they could minimize wait times on this busy day and which cars might need to be cleaned first. On his return to the front desk, he asks one of the service center agents to accompany him and they go through a similar routine of talking and questioning.

It's little things like this that help Aguilera keep his people energized. He communicates well, he trusts others' judgment, and he spends an inordinate amount of time with his high-potential people to make sure they stay.

One last example of energizing, this time from Chick-fil-A.

Restaurateur Truett Cathy founded this chain of chicken restaurants in the 1960s with a goal of running a family business with principles and values. Chick-fil-A still considers itself a small family culture, and yet the results are anything but small. It has seen 43 consecutive years of sales growth. At year-end 2010, annual sales were more than $3.5 billion, with more than 1,500 locations. It is the second-largest fast-food chicken restaurant in the United States, after Kentucky Fried Chicken.

True to his father's legacy, President and COO Dan Cathy loves to add service touches that people don't expect from a fast-food restaurant. As such, he encourages Chick-fil-A's independent owner/operators to ask their team members to fold the last sheet of toilet paper into a triangular point after they clean the restrooms or say "My pleasure" whenever a customer thanks them.

More pertinent to our discussion, Andy Lorenzen, director of talent strategy, said, "Our restaurants are unexpectedly energized places to work, socialize, and eat."

One way the chain maintains that kind of energy is by setting clear expectations and ensuring people feel recognized when they uphold high standards. For instance, team members rush to fill orders within two minutes at the drive-through window and under a minute at the counter. A timer on a monitor flashes yellow if an order is in jeopardy of going over time; the timer turns red if it does and the crew goes crazy. Owners create a daily sense of competitiveness among the crews and then reward the best. In Louisville, Kentucky, owner/operator Chris Flanagan erected a big red "drive-through wall of fame" to motivate his people. It lists the current record (110 cars in an hour) and the names of those who achieved it. Whenever a team sets a new mark, he presents each member with an award and a new plaque goes up.

Can you say energizing?

The resulting growth of the company has certainly been phenomenal, but its reputation for maintaining work-life balance is legendary. In fact, when some people are asked about Chick-fil-A, they admit the first thing that comes to mind is that the stores are closed on Sundays. Said Lorenzen, "If we say our greatest assets are our people—owner/operators and their team members—we think closing doors on Sundays is the least we can do to show that we also value their families too."

Senior Vice President of Operations Tim Tassopoulos began working for Chick-fil-A (CFA) in 1977 as an hourly team member in Atlanta. He stayed through college and graduate school. Tassopoulos joked with us that it's harder to become an owner/operator with CFA than it is to join the CIA. "Annually we have about twelve thousand people who express interest in becoming a Chick-fil-A operator, and we chose about seventy to ninety. It's unbelievably selective. We focus on a person's track record, not just their business performance, but their track record in their community, their ability to lead and inspire a team, their character."

Chick-fil-A is first and foremost looking for leaders who exemplify the values of the culture, trustworthy people who can help energize employees with the strength of their character.

Said Dan Cathy, "The ideal Chick-fil-A leader is a servant to their staff, not a leader who wants his staff to be his servants. Our managers treat their employees they way they want those employees, in turn, to treat customers."

Thus, interviews to become an owner/operator can take more

than a year. Said Tassopoulos, "Fundamentally the question we ask before we go into business with an independent owner/operator is, *Would we want our children to go to work for this person?*" Think about that: Leaders have actually humanized the process of identifying potential partners and put it into terms that everyone can understand. But there's more. After papers are finally signed for a new franchise, these individuals undergo extensive training in Atlanta, which includes time with the Cathy family, who conduct vision and values briefings at their homes.

"You have to believe there is a higher purpose to your work," said Tassopoulos, summing up Chick-fil-A's approach to culture. "There's no question for me, a principle-centered, values-centered organization can literally change people's lives. When customers see how committed we are to giving back to our people and our communities, they want to support our business. Does it get any better than that?"

Of course as important as energizing is to a company's success, it's just one part of the equation. The true power comes from the triad: engagement, enablement, and energy. Towers Watson has found companies with the combined impact of all three factors can generate operating margins three times higher than companies with low engagement, and nearly two times higher than companies with high engagement alone.

Said Patrick Kulesa, global research director in Towers Watson's employee survey practice, "We find in the exponential-engagement culture the elements that underpin top performance. The data clearly shows that to fire up your people to participate in the success of the business, leaders must set the tone. They must create a personal connection to what the business is doing and how it is changing with the times, create an open and high-trust environment, and retain the best people—from the CEO down to an entry-level person. Good leaders drive culture. Good cultures attract good people who understand where they fit and that they can grow. Leaders unlock that potential."

*   *   *

What follows is a good schematic for summarizing the importance of the E + E + E idea.

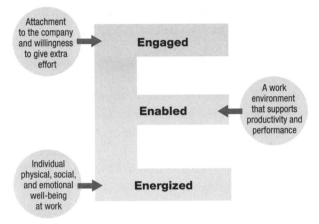

The key elements of exponential engagement according to Towers Watson, 2011.

≈ ALL IN ≈

DYSFUNCTIONAL CULTURES

The sad truth is that many workplaces do not display the characteristics we've outlined above. There are dysfunctional cultures—those permeated by negativity and defeatism, lack of accountability, blame and backstabbing, lack of vision or focus, dictatorial management, secrecy, rigidity . . . we could go on and on, and so could you. The question is, where does your culture stand? Below we have taken some of the most common dysfunctions and placed them in a test to help you determine if your culture has toxic elements. We recommend taking this survey in two ways—by placing a check mark near the ideas that in your opinion apply to your overall company culture, and then by putting yourself in the position of your employees and placing an X next to the ideas that they would say apply to your team.

Note that a passing grade on this quiz should be zero, though we might allow one or two checkmarks or Xs before the alarm bells sound.

The Dysfunctional Culture Quiz

❏ Leaders around here don't seem very focused on challenges and opportunities that are coming down the road.

❏ We place too much emphasis on short-term results or getting our bonuses, often at the expense of investing for growth.

❏ Our environment has more than its fair share of backstabbing, faultfinding, and idea-stealing.

❏ Negative client comments are hidden from view. And when clients are angry or we lose one, leaders don't try very hard to understand the root causes.

❏ There's little accountability around here, and/or we are judged by less than high standards.

❏ Teams don't cross boundaries to work together; we have a silo mentality.

❏ There's not a lot of trust in management; it's us versus them.

❏ We have little sense of urgency to improve; leaders seem to think everything is pretty good the way it is.

❏ There have not been many good new ideas floating around lately.

❏ Much of the time we don't know what's going on in corporate or even in our own department.

❏ We aren't known for giving real feedback or having tough discussions. I don't feel like I could give my boss honest criticism, for instance.

❏ There's a lot of attention given to our past victories instead of honestly assessing our current situation.

❏ We don't celebrate successes very often.

❏ Our best people seem to be leaving.

The quiz contains fourteen hard questions to ask yourself about your culture. If you checked more than a few boxes, it's time for some serious introspection and work. If you checked four or more of these problems, your culture is probably on life support or about to suffer some serious health issues. You need to fix things, and fast.

The good news is this: There are changes you can make in the coming months that will have a big impact.

Let's go back to the American Express atrium in Fort Lauderdale for a last thought.

Doria Camaraza has a tradition with long-tenured employees who are retiring. She takes a final walk with them. She thanks them on behalf of the company for all their years of service. And then on cue, people six floors up approach the atrium balconies and give their friend one last standing ovation.

"People are crying, including me," she said. "And after the round of applause I ceremonially walk them to the turnstile."

Good beginnings. Good endings. There is something beautiful in that moment, in the attention Camaraza pays to not only those who join but those who leave. It is civilized and decent, but it also is culture at its most powerful.

Camaraza and her leadership team are good managers, but they are not Supermen and Superwomen. They work hard and efficiently, but then they go home to their families and to volunteer work they love.

What they have learned to do has been just that, learned. It can be replicated. And that tells us any leader can achieve similar results. The question, of course, is how. Can you learn how to inspire people to follow you? Can you learn how to get your people all in?

You can, by following the steps we'll now introduce in more detail.

PART II

The Seven-Step Road Map

How Every Manager Can Create
a Culture That Works

4

Define Your Burning Platform

Supply the Why

Not long ago, General Motors ruled the U.S. car market. It was without peer. At its competitive height, fifty years ago, GM made and sold 54 percent of all vehicles on U.S. roads. In the mid-1970s, a still-whopping 47 percent of cars and trucks bought by American consumers were manufactured by GM. That kind of market share—owning half the cars on the road—created understandable feelings of security and superiority in Detroit.

But, as we know now, things were about to change.

An oil embargo in 1973 doubled the price of gas from thirty cents a gallon almost overnight; a second embargo six years later pushed the cost of crude up even farther; and by 1980, the price was ninety cents a gallon. American motorists became understandably interested in more fuel-efficient vehicles, and the most popular were small, well-built Japanese models. GM did respond to the competitive threat by making some smaller cars too, but consumers generally believed they paled in comparison. GM's market share began to slip, but the retreat was glacially slow—about 1 percent per year. By the mid-1980s, more than one in three vehicles sold domestically was still a GM; in fact the company's revenue remained larger than most countries' entire GDP, and in 1984, GM posted a record annual profit of $4.52 billion.

Still, executives realized it was time to offer a better small car to their consumers. So in 1984, General Motors opened a joint venture in Fremont, California, called New United Motor Manufacturing Incorporated (NUMMI). Their partner was an upstart Japanese company called Toyota. Starting in the mid-1960s, Toyota had gained a reputation for its ability to control costs and improve quality—ironically, using the philosophies of American Edwards Deming. But the company was still relatively small, and the pairing of an American powerhouse and a Japanese upstart was scandalous. At the time, GM was seven times larger than Toyota. A headline in *Car and Driver* magazine read HELL FREEZES OVER.

True to its word, Toyota showed GM how it achieved such quality, how it got workers to take ownership, and how management and employees operated as a team. Analysts predicted GM would learn the Toyota production system and take the ideas into plants around the globe, improving efficiency and quality.

It didn't.

Says Jeffrey Liker, University of Michigan engineering professor and author of *The Toyota Way*, General Motors didn't appear particularly interested. "I'm not sure it was a hundred percent accepted by GM senior management that Japanese quality was really better."

This hubris wasn't GM's alone. Liker asserts that many at the Big Three U.S. automakers "believed that if the American consumer thinks we have quality issues it's because *Consumer Reports* is misleading them. They are biased toward Toyota. There was a myth of Japanese quality." Liker says, "I think there was pride and defensiveness. 'I'm proud because I'm the biggest. You can't teach me anything, you little Japanese company.'"

Realistically, it would have taken a Herculean effort to implement the Japanese system of teamwork, empowerment, and continuous improvement at GM, a company so large, compartmentalized, and complex. First, workers were distrustful of the Japanese efficiency gains—weren't they simply a way for senior leadership to lay off a large portion of the workforce?

In addition, many middle managers were troubled by a system that would give employees a powerful voice—including the right to stop the production line if they saw problems and even the right to park their personal cars just as close to the building as managers (believe it or not, a fact that bothered many). As for senior executives, they were busy, very busy. They were managing acquisitions such as EDS and Hughes Aircraft, they had just launched the marketing machine that was Saturn, and they were negotiating complicated union contracts with their line workers.

A transformation of GM would certainly have been monumental, but it would not have been impossible. And yet the improvements didn't happen in the 1980s for one significant reason: No one at GM had a sense of urgency about the Japanese threat. Liker asserts that GM executives simply didn't believe the company was in trouble. It was. And in 1992 the wheels came off. That year GM lost more than $23.5 billion, the largest loss by any company in the history of American business. A new CEO was put in place with a new agenda: to install a NUMMI-like production system around the organization. Progress was made, but it took time—almost another decade, in fact—before GM and its unions had finalized the Global Manufacturing System.

The problem was, GM had to turn around a battleship with a paddle. It worked, says Liker, it just took a long time. "You are seeing a level of quality you didn't see fifteen years ago." (Indeed, one of the authors is very pleased with his Chevy.)

If that turnaround had been managed with more urgency, the Great Recession of 2008 might not have driven GM into bankruptcy. To recover, the company required $19 billion in loans and $30 billion in financing, and half of its factories were closed, with some 20,000 workers being fired and thousands of dealerships shut down. Parts distribution warehouses, engine plants, a stamping plant, and assembly lines for Pontiac and Saturn were closed. Hummer and Saab were also shed.

That same year Toyota became the world's largest automaker, and GM's market share in the U.S. hit a rock-bottom 19 percent.

To be fair, some of the causes for GM's implosion were out of its control—deregulation of domestic oil prices, a ban on Iranian oil imports, an onslaught of small-car manufacturers around the world, economic cycles of boom and bust, rapid increases in health care and other costs such as pension responsibilities. Still, its competitors faced the same market drivers and some managed to not only survive but steal market share.

The fact is that for a long time, some pundits claimed GM wasn't really in the car production business at all. The side that really made money was GMAC, the car-loan-financing arm. For years, a running joke was that GM was a bank that made cars on the side. Finance's success masked troubles in the plants much longer than would have otherwise been possible.

Unfortunately, as the credit crisis hit (GMAC was also in the mortgage business), General Motors suddenly was unable to help potential buyers as it had before. And dealerships couldn't finance inventory either. It was a perfect storm of bad news.

"One of the ironies of GM was that in the moment it went bankrupt it was probably a better company than it had ever been," says James Womack, author of *The Machine That Changed the World*. "In the factories they had really dramatically closed the productivity gap they had for many years, and on the new products they had much better quality. But it was too late. If you take thirty years to figure it out, you'll get run over."

Experts argue about what brought GM to such a low place. Was it that focus on financing strategies versus innovation, higher production costs and ballooning health care expenses, a bet on gas-guzzling vehicles such as the Hummer line, and the decision to scrap the EV1 electric car in testing? All played a role, but, in reality, GM almost certainly would have turned itself around much sooner if only an influential voice of urgency had arisen within the company. It lacked a voice of warning— which rival Ford had in its executive team, allowing it to escape government bailout.

Please don't construe this as saying that the company's troubles were the result of a lack of intelligence. On the contrary, GM executives ran one of the most complicated organizations on the planet. They were quite smart. No, what they suffered from was *contentment*. What General Motors needed was someone yelling as loud and long as it took to make everyone understand that their platform was on fire.

What do we mean by a "burning platform"? The term derives from the following story. A man working on an oil rig in the North Sea was awakened suddenly one night by an explosion. Amid the chaos, he made his way to the edge of the platform. As a plume of fire billowed behind him, he realized he needed to take the plunge into the icy sea—some five stories below. The water was littered with smoldering debris and oil, not to mention icy cold and a thousand feet deep, but the man survived the long drop and the swim in the raging sea. He was eventually hauled aboard a rescue boat. When asked why he jumped into uncertainty, he replied, "Better probable death than certain death."

The point: Only the literal "burning platform" could cause such a radical change in his behavior.

Your team may not be running for its life, but with competition much, much fiercer these days, you undoubtedly face issues that threaten your livelihood and your organization's very survival. (There is nothing quite as sobering as reading a list of the leading companies of two decades ago to see how few of them exist today.) Your ability to identify and define the key "burning" issue you face and separate it from the routine challenges of the day is the first step in galvanizing your employees to believe in you and in your vision and strategy.

If this talk about jumping from an oil derrick seems a tad dramatic for you, understand that most people will change only when their survival anxiety is greater than the apprehension they face about learning something new. Though we do have an insatiable curiosity for the new and we tend to like the excitement of a challenge, we also like to be comfortable in our work environments. Contentment typically wins out in the long run, and most people naturally gravitate toward a stasis and emotional equilibrium on the job. We like safety, especially when our livelihoods are at stake. This is where survival anxiety comes into play; it drives home the painful realization that in order to succeed we have to change.

That's why every leader must explain in very clear terms to their teams why they must step up and refocus their efforts, all while creating a reassuringly safe environment. Helping employees understand they're on a burning platform is not about fear, but more about framing the conversation in honest and real terms that employees can relate to. Remember, for instance, Starbucks CEO Howard Schultz's jarring 800-word e-mail to all Starbucks employees in which he claimed his company was losing the "romance and theatre" so core to its defining DNA. Or consider the so-called Peanut Butter Manifesto issued by Brad Garlinghouse, then a senior VP at Yahoo!, who sent a memo to his entire company warning that they were spreading themselves too thin and losing focus. Warnings of this kind have grown in frequency and, with social media and e-mail, are increasingly becoming public. In the cases of Starbucks and Yahoo!, the executives painted an honest assessment of their current situations, but each also expressed a sincere belief that their team had the talent to rally.

If General Motors had developed this kind of clarity and understanding in the eighties as competition heated up, if leaders had seen that their platform was burning and realized the urgency to develop the quality system the company runs on now, more consumers would have trusted its vehicles and its share of the road most likely would not have eroded so severely. Of course, in the case of GM, the story is not over yet, and we wish them well. We also hope that others can learn from their mistake. We can't count the number of times we've heard leaders glibly claim something such as, "Sales are up four percent this year," while not admitting even under cross-examination that their net income is down, margins are eroding, and the industry as a whole is growing at twice their pace.

We begin our dialogue with such smart but content managers with the simple questions we will pose to you now:

- Why is it imperative that your people buy into your strategy? (Define your threats on the horizon and begin outlining why you're on a burning platform.)
- What do you do, and why do you do it? (What is your mission?)
- Whom do you do it for? (Who are your customers?)
- How will you get where you want to go? (What are your values and goals?)

No matter the size of your team or the challenges you face, it is the job of leaders to help their people understand why it's not acceptable to remain where you are, that you must move toward a better future, and why it's safe to do so, much safer than not doing so. Wise leaders often prove the point dramatically—showing employees the benefits of a competitor's products, illustrating firsthand how some customers view their underwhelming level of customer service, or even providing that list of companies of a few decades ago and asking employees to identify how many still exist today.

Leaders then must provide clarity around what the company does and why it does it, whom it does it for, and the ways their employees are going to collectively reach their goals—all down to the level of each individual's job. The progression is captured in this simple process model.

WHERE DO MANAGERS GO WRONG?

There should be nothing revelatory in that graphic. Yet we've probably all seen the ideas of mission, values, and goals implemented so poorly it made us want to laugh, or cry. The fact is much of the time communication of these ideas is done badly. Employees in one company showed us a slick wallet card and other stylized messages from the executive team—complete with their values and mission—and admitted to us that they had cynically dubbed these guiding principles "motherhood and apple pie." Culture isn't about slick marketing or cool design, and in this company the ideas never caught on.

In a dot-com firm we began working with, the head of one business unit told us our visit was fortuitous since the leadership team had just come up with its first set of values. When we asked him to recite the values, he excused himself to run back to his office for a written copy of them (never a good sign). When he returned to our meeting room, he proudly showed us the twelve grand principles he and his fellow executives had written. We had to remind him that Moses only had ten commandments, and most people don't remember those either.

Here are a few steps to follow to avoid pessimism, at least for the vast majority of your people, and increase retention of these ideas: Keep your mission simple and aspirational, and your values to a manageable list—three is ideal, with five as a maximum. Next, you should also give, if possible, every person a small voice in deciding the mission and values, but certainly a larger role in determining goals and expectations, or in other words, what all these grand ideas mean to their teams, their jobs, and their future—fueling pride and creating momentum that builds as employees reach milestones along the way.

When leaders work to establish mission, values, and goals, they must realize they face an equal chance of one of three eventualities: adoption, oblivion, or backfire. *Adoption* requires an extensive process of employee input, management accountability, and continuing messaging and training. It is rare.

Most common is *oblivion,* as the majority of such ideas and priorities are never integrated into the corporate culture but fade away, victims of subpar or inconsistent communication. Where many managers slip up is trying to focus their employees as if this process were something to check off a to-do list rather than a commitment that runs DNA-deep. Superficiality in this process is deadly, because employees mirror it. They view your mission, core values, and goals as things to outlast rather than to embrace.

Another common cause of oblivion we encounter is a focus on a goal or set of goals that is impossible to attain. In these cases, managers reason that if business objectives are extremely difficult, even unreasonable, employees will be energized to push themselves to great lengths, well beyond their normal efforts. In actuality, most employees reason that if goals can't really be met, there's no point in even trying.

At the other end of the continuum are managers who believe that goals should be challenging, but all employees should be equally rewarded if the goal is reached, despite individual contributions. *We're all in this together,* they reason. When employees see colleagues exerting little or no effort and still achieving an equal reward, the message is clear: Striving for greatness is not rewarded.

A *backfire* is more problematic than oblivion. Most often this reaction is triggered by an inconsistency between the values being espoused and the way that leaders themselves act. Consider this example we heard from a marketing employee at a large firm we'll keep confidential. Company leadership had unveiled a new values statement that included the well-intended, artfully crafted notion that "feedback is a gift." Just days later, leaders received the results of an employee survey showing a precipitous dive in scores on the statement, "My manager is open to feedback."

The timing couldn't have been worse for the executive team. With a series of all-hands meetings just two weeks away—where the most senior leaders would meet in small groups with every employee in the company—leadership found themselves grappling with two competing priorities: the desire to avoid further (almost certainly negative) employee feedback on the issue and their responsibility to model the acceptance of feedback as a gift and opportunity for improvement.

With gallows humor, the employee we spoke with said her marketing colleagues were joking behind the scenes, "What we meant to say was 'Our feedback to you is a gift, yours you can keep.'"

Over the next two weeks, leaders considered six separate approaches to spinning the issue of the poor feedback scores, complete with six sets of slides developed by marketing employees. This team pulled all-nighters trying to make a proverbial silk purse out of a pig's ear.

In the end, on the day of the first group meeting, the designated senior manager did the right thing. She stood before one of the most vocal groups in the organization, shut off the projector, and presented the survey data without any spin. She explained what management had discovered, what they would do, and what changes to expect in the future. "They'll be baby steps at first," she said, "but we did listen and we aren't going to ignore this feedback." And then she opened the room up to questions. While several employees immediately spoke out angrily, other workers raised their hands to counter their teammates' complaints. The leader had to say very little more on the issue except to thank employees for their honest comments and to assure them that the leadership team was finally heeding the advice.

In this case, a wise leader helped reinforce one of the company's core values—listening to one another. A potential backfire became the first step toward adoption. And, as an aside, while certain divisions of this company have continued to stumble at times in living this value, when we got an update from the marketing employee she told us overall feedback scores a year later were indeed higher, which has led to improved survey results in areas such as employee trust and engagement.

≈ ALL IN ≈

FIRST THE WHY

For many years now it has been an established part of business lore that articulating a clear and appealing mission and set of values, with authenticity of managerial commitment to them, produces powerful results. A foundational story in the history of this wisdom is that of Lincoln Electric, a welding supply company founded in 1895. John Lincoln, and later his younger brother James, were among the first to use modern leadership techniques to achieve success, pioneers in taking a mission, values, and goals and turning them into something employees would really care about on an individual level, spurring not one or two but seven *Harvard Business Review* case studies on this outwardly unexciting supplier of welding supply products.

Shortly after the company opened, Lincoln hung a thirty-foot sign over his factory door that proclaimed THE ACTUAL IS LIMITED. THE POSSIBLE IS IMMENSE, and the workers who daily passed below this sign found that Lincoln and other leaders not only believed in that spirit of innovation, they really lived it. Although commodity costs soared following the Great Depression and continued upward through World War II into the early 1970s, Lincoln Electric's mission of continuous improvement kept their product prices much lower than their competitors'. While material costs tripled, its prices increased by only 50 percent. Obviously to achieve this the company vastly improved productivity—more than doubling the output of the rest of the industry.

The company's leaders created a sharp focus on a set of guiding principles, values, and goals down to the individual worker's level. It was a manager's first responsibility to make the mission clear for each employee: produce more of a progressively better product at a lower price for a larger group of customers. In short: make more, improve quality, cut costs, sell more. Each employee's earnings and promotions would be in direct correlation to his individual contribution toward this big goal, an idea that created a lot of buzz at the time. To encourage teamwork, a year-end bonus, which at least equaled the individual's annual pay, was paid based on dependability, quality, output, ideas, and cooperation. To incentivize *individual* productivity, wages in the factory were based on piecework.

The benefits were clear. In 1974, when the median income for U.S. manufacturing employees was less than $9,200, this compensation plan resulted in some industrious Lincoln Electric hourly workers earning more than $45,000 (which would be about $200,000 in today's dollars). At the peak of the company's success in the mid-1970s, even the shipping department was receiving attention from the business press. Employee ideas had cut costs substantially by consolidating orders. That meant 90 percent of orders went out in full carloads or truckloads. If a train gave the same rate for twenty thousand to forty thousand pounds, then employees would ensure that the car left with forty thousand pounds of products to capitalize on the lower rate. It might not sound like a cutting-edge strategy today, but forty years ago this kind of efficiency was not at all common. Operating "lean" simply wasn't a priority in American business. But Lincoln Electric rewarded its employees individually and collectively for accomplishing it.

Today, high-performing leaders have a similar almost maniacal level of focus on their mission. But their greatest urgency is not on managing operational details but on establishing employee priorities. It's something race car drivers know by heart: Where the eyes go, the car goes. Similarly, managers of high-performance teams never take their eyes off the goal, and they make sure their employees are keeping their eyes on it too.

During our interviews with high-performance leaders, each displayed a dogged commitment to their mission and core set of values, and each provided a clear direction for their group— no matter the size of the team or organization, no matter the industry. But color was added to this when we asked individual contributors in high-performance cultures about their leaders.

They would say things such as, "He forces us to think of the big picture," or "She reminds us that real people use our products, and they have to be perfect every time." The question is, do you provide that kind of clarity in your leadership style, or do you assume such grand direction should come from corporate?

There is an art to how high-performing leaders articulate their mission that gives employees the vital understanding of their place within the organization's larger cause. It is a humanizing process that helps a work group building, say, portable basketball standards to believe they are providing a way for families to spend more quality time together, or a team refurbishing tractor engines to feel as if they are keeping costs low for farmers and thereby providing affordable food for those in need.

Tremendous motivational power comes with tapping into universally held ideals in this way. And once the link is made between a company mission and a value an employee holds dear, the positive emotions are transferred to the employee's work. People commit more energetically to what you are doing because they believe in it personally.

Take this striking example of the power of inspiring a key employee with a larger mission that resonated for him: Just four years after founding Apple in a garage, Steve Jobs realized he needed a more orthodox chief executive to run the company, a respectable face who could sell to corporate America. He didn't aim low. In 1983, he offered the job to one of the business world's rising stars: John Sculley, president of PepsiCo, the man who had introduced the Pepsi Challenge and other marketing innovations to the soda company. Sculley politely refused the offer—after all, he had a pretty sweet deal at Pepsi corporate. He was the company's youngest-ever president, Pepsi was growing under his leadership, and his compensation plan would undoubtedly make him wealthy before his first gray hairs arrived. But it was hard saying no to Steve Jobs.

Sculley described what followed: "He looked up at me and just stared at me with the stare that only Steve Jobs had and he said, 'Come with me and change the world,' and I just gulped because I knew I would wonder for the rest of my life what I would have missed."

In that moment, in no uncertain terms, Jobs linked Sculley's work at Apple to something larger in scope than the job he was doing. Pepsi offers a product that people love, no doubt, but in 1983 the personal computer was on the cusp of changing the entire world. The appeal worked, and the man who helped introduce the world-famous Pepsi Challenge went to work for the start-up computer company—and changed its trajectory. During Sculley's tenure in the 1980s and 1990s, Apple's sales increased from $800 million to $8 billion.

≈ ALL IN ≈

THE PEPSI CHALLENGE

To see how effective the process of articulating mission, values, and goals can be when done right, we'll look at another story surrounding the powerful Pepsi brand. Let us take you back to 1999. That year PepsiCo divested itself of its bottling division, Pepsi Bottling Group (PBG), in what was one of the largest-ever initial public offerings in the history of the New York Stock Exchange. The bottling company would instantly become the world's largest distributor of Pepsi drinks, with 70,000 employees bottling and selling more than 40 percent of Pepsi beverages worldwide—about 200 million servings a day.

In reality, as an investment, PBG had a lot going against it. It was a big, unsexy bottling company—stuck smack-dab in the middle of a mature industry with increasing competition from bottled waters, vitamin drinks, juices, and the greatest selection of beverage choices in the history of consumerism. And at first blush it didn't seem like a place that could attract the best talent. After all, employees had the seemingly mundane job of loading soda onto trucks and delivering the bottles and cans to convenience stores and supermarkets. They weren't rushing into burning buildings to save lives or teaching inner-city kids to read; they were making people less thirsty.

And yet Pepsi Bottling Group defied the odds. Leaders found a way to create a culture where employees had a fierce resolve to "pour it on" every day. Profitability went through the roof. In the ten years following its IPO, Pepsi Bottling Group would almost double in size from $8 billion in annual sales to $15 billion, and the stock price would appreciate by 330 percent. It is a success story in rarified company.

But as in most good yarns, the company had a rocky start. Just months after the launch, the stock was trading at 25 percent less than the IPO price. The platform was smoldering. Wall Street wasn't buying into the company's direction, and when shareholders aren't happy, people tend to lose their jobs. Can you imagine the urgency building at headquarters?

John Berisford was senior vice president of human resources during the IPO and the decade that followed. He says, "In the dark days of 2000, when the stock was at its lowest, in that seminal moment, we knew the market was telling us they didn't buy our strategy. Since we were a spin-off we already had customers, products, trucks, forklifts. The work of creating a purpose or mission statement didn't seem that critical to some. It was."

A group of leaders put together some ideas for a mission and values to bind this new company together, and they brought those to Craig Weatherup, PBG's new chairman and CEO. Weatherup had just returned from a visit to Denver, where he'd spoken with a shrewd delivery driver. The chairman had asked the man a series of questions, including, "What do you do?" "How do you do it?" and "What help do you want from headquarters to do your job?"

The driver's answers were succinct, and at one point he said, "You know, Craig, you guys make things so complicated. It's really not that hard. We sell soda."

The simplicity struck Weatherup, and he encouraged the mission group to consider "We Sell Soda" as not only PBG's mission but also its rallying cry.

Up to that point, explains Berisford, Pepsi Bottling Group had been a culture of individual heroics, of solitary route salesmen trying to outsell the guys in the red trucks. "But that little word 'we,' that simple word, became critical. We all began to think about the supply chain in total. Do the concentrate shipments arrive when they should, what happens when they show up at the manufacturing facility, how does manufacturing produce a high-quality product on time, how does it get loaded on the trucks?"

PBG began moving from a culture of "I" to a culture of "we."

The second word, "sell," galvanized the team around passionate salesmanship and service. For instance, it became the first consumer-product goods company to satisfy a need for paperless pallets at retail giant Walmart, which dramatically reduced inventory checks for this important client. "We began with a customer need, and then we'd massively reengineer to take all of the bottlenecks and inefficiency out of our system," Berisford said.

Finally, the word "soda" reminded them of the core product offering and focused everyone in the company on what they did best. Said Berisford, "Without the word 'soda' in our mission, the executive team might seriously have thought about putting chewing gum or other items on our trucks. It would have made sense; our drivers were going to the stores anyway. But it would have complicated our business, and we would not have provided the level of focused service our customers wanted. We wouldn't have grown like we did."

Those three words, "We Sell Soda," gave PBG laser focus. But that wasn't all the PBG leadership did; they also established four operating principles, or values, which they called the Rules of the Road:

1. Drive Local Market Success.
2. Act Now. Do It Today. Get Results.
3. Set Targets. Keep Score. Win.
4. Respect Each Other.

Berisford explains, "The rules were our core values, and they helped us establish goals and expectations down to the individual route level. In Allensville, West Virginia, the route driver had specific expectations born from the four rules. And in a universe with hundreds of thousands of customers, he could determine in a moment whether Paul's Bait Shop got the seven cases of Pepsi they ordered. If they didn't, drivers were asked to follow the principle that they should 'solve it by sundown.'" For instance, that often meant industrious drivers would drive back to the distribution center to grab additional product instead of waiting a day or two for a return visit to a customer—certainly impressive to those clients and their thirsty patrons.

PBG drivers like this weren't just filling up soda coolers, they were working hard to ensure that the company fulfilled its mission. "In a big company or small, people want to believe that their work is important," says Berisford. "For that inspiration, they look to see what their leaders believe. If the territory manager in Dodge City, Kansas, believes his mission is to zealously serve his customers and sell more of our amazing soda, it becomes contagious."

And thus, purpose became more important than the immediate financials. For instance, if a PBG manager missed his or her financial targets for four straight quarters, but they were enrolled in the mission and values of the company, they would not only survive but most likely flourish. "What we looked for in our leaders was values and character and inspiring others. Even when certain of our people weren't winning by the numbers, we continued to recognize them for living our values because we knew it was the right thing to do. And eventually they started to turn."

PBG's values and purpose kept them on a strong growth track for a decade. And when it eventually made sense to bring Pepsi Bottling Group and PepsiCo back together, PBG leaders insisted on keeping their mission and values at their new division, renamed Pepsi Beverages Company.

≈ ALL IN ≈

ARE THEY SNEEZEABLE?

Effective managers manifest their commitment to mission and values in everything they do—their actions, their dreams, their example, and certainly their speech. As our friends Jim Kouzes and Barry Posner said in their classic *The Leadership Challenge,* "There's nothing more demoralizing than a leader who can't clearly articulate why we're doing what we're doing."

We've probably all worked for a manager who is good at the how of work but doesn't help us understand the why. He might stress safety, for instance, because it's a corporate policy, but he doesn't remind us that if we tie off our ladders and wear our hard hats it will help us go home to our families every night, or that we are impacting more junior workers with our example.

With any behavior, any product offered, any service, a good manager should be able to explain *why* the action is necessary and *whom* it impacts. No matter the size of the group they manage, great leaders understand their first responsibility is not to margin or procedure, but to translate the ethereal corporate mission into day-to-day priorities for their people. They first identify the potential precipitous decline on the horizon as the burning platform to change. They motivate others by reminding them of the view of a better future and by providing the clear goals, values, and expectations associated with their role in helping fulfill the bigger mission, and, in turn, employees focus their energies on the tasks with the most impact. As a result, financial results can multiply.

Few places have embodied this process in our minds better than the American Express World Service Center in Fort Lauderdale we profiled in chapter 3. Every month about fourteen people start their first day there. These wide-eyed new recruits spend a few minutes chatting with General Manager Doria Camaraza, and then they line up to get their identification badges. It takes about fifteen minutes to process everyone, and the wait is on purpose. Next to the security station is a six-foot-high lighted box displaying a list of the eight company values—such as "A Will to Win," "Teamwork," and "Integrity." A new employee has little to do but read the values and their definitions and soak in the fact that they'll not only be serving customers but each other.

Here, the process of understanding "why we do what we do" begins on day one.

Steve Gaswirth is the center's vice president of service engineering and transformation. He says, "I don't like the mushroom theory that many managers subscribe to. They put people in a dark room and dump fertilizer on them. People can't be kept in the dark. They've got to connect the relevance of their efforts to business outcomes. When they deliver a project and cash registers start ringing or we reduce expenses or we increase customer satisfaction, they can see how it achieves goals; that's a great motivator."

Of course American Express is not unique in having core values—most businesses have them—but what is exceptional in this facility is the inordinate amount of time leaders spend helping employees understand why these operating principles are so important to their collective success. They have made their mission and values "sneezeable."

It doesn't matter if you run a department in a hospital, manage a team at an airline, or paint the beaks on rubber chickens; you spread mission and values in much the same way a sneeze travels. Think about this: How do you catch a cold? First, someone sneezes into his hand and grabs a doorknob. You come along and touch the doorknob and boom, chicken soup and Zicam. Later you sneeze and spread your cold in a movie theater, on an airplane, or at your local Wienerschnitzel. Pretty soon folks in Topeka and Taiwan have caught the same bug. One sneeze has gone global.

Mission and values can spread just as fast throughout an organization if they are authentic and provide real meaning for employees. The American Express values, such as "respect for people" and "personal accountability," aren't particularly zany like some we've seen, but they are extremely relevant to the behind-the-scenes work of serving the needs of credit card holders.

This might be a good time to ask yourself: Do your mission and values provide a larger purpose for your employees? Are they forgettable or genuine and striking? Do we spread them effectively and consistently every single day?

After all, the most important element of spreading the sneezeable ideas of mission and values is connecting with those in your care on a regular basis. "You've got to open your door and connect with people to help them understand how important their work is to the organization," says Gaswirth. "I can't just get a five-minute update once every few weeks from my people; I have to work to understand what they are working on and how I might help solve their problems. If they are in a distant location I use tools like video conferencing and project reviews."

In short, identifying that you're on a burning platform provides urgency. Mission drives clarity about why we do what we do. Values offer the ways we work together. And goals provide the steps and timelines to success. It is a process of looking forward, even if only a few minutes or hours into the future, to help a team member understand why she should care. This is a foundational step that can lead a manager to breakthrough results, but only if you focus in the right direction. Always, always, these ideas come not from looking inward but from looking outward to the needs of the customers. That's where the research takes us next.

Step Summary

DEFINE YOUR BURNING PLATFORM
SUPPLY THE WHY

- It is not a lack of intelligence that sinks cultures, but contentment.
- Your ability to identify and define the key "burning" issue you face and separate it from the routine challenges of the day is the first step in galvanizing your employees to believe in you and your vision and strategy.
- Most people will change only when their survival anxiety is greater than the apprehension they face about learning something new.
- Helping employees understand they're on a burning platform is not about fear but about framing the conversation in honest and real terms that employees can relate to.
- Leaders provide clarity around what you do and why, whom you do it for, and the ways you are going to collectively reach your goals—all down to the level of each individual's job.
- Keep your mission simple and inspirational and your values to a manageable list. If possible, give people a voice in determining those bigger ideas, but always a larger role in determining team goals and individual expectations.
- High-performing leaders' greatest urgency is on establishing employee priorities. It's something race car drivers know by heart: Where the eyes go, the car goes.
- Mission and values can be sneezeable if they are authentic and provide real meaning for employees.
- Ask yourself: Do your mission and values provide a larger purpose? Are they forgettable or genuine and striking? Do you spread them effectively and consistently every day?

5

Create a Customer Focus

Are You Listening?

It seems clear to most of us now that if General Motors had listened to their customers in the 1980s, the company may not have suffered such an ignominious bankruptcy. According to Peter Cohan of Babson College, "General Motors had been ignoring competition for decades. Toyota and its peers took over GM's market share because they offered a better car-buying and -ownership experience."

Many of us are driving down a similar road. We are oblivious to what customers find attractive about our rivals; we live in a self-reverential bliss. It's a decades-old trend. Not only GM but many of the world's top companies from the mid-1980s have foundered, shrunk, grown obsolete, or been acquired by rivals that grew stronger. Digital Equipment and Wang Laboratories, once leading computer firms, disappeared completely. Even resurgent titans like Apple and IBM stared into the abyss of irrelevance and had to make painful changes before clawing their way back to the top.

Most companies, of course, never get to the top, and the few that do find it daunting to stay there. Vijay Govindarajan, professor at Dartmouth's Tuck School of Business and coauthor of *The Other Side of Innovation,* teaches that successful companies tend to fall into traps that make the glory days fleeting. First is the physical trap, in which big investments in old systems or equipment prevent the pursuit of fresher, more relevant investments. There's the strategic trap, when a company focuses purely on the marketplace of today and fails to anticipate the future. And then there's a psychological trap, in which company leaders fixate on what made them successful and fail to notice when something new is displacing it. He says some unlucky companies even manage a trifecta and fall into all three traps.

Of course, it's not always as obvious where your competition is coming from or what your customers want as it was for GM. The company or idea that could threaten your very survival may not even be on your radar yet, but the best leaders encourage everyone on their team to be on a vigilant watch for disruptive solutions or trends that might harm their firm. Unfortunately too many companies fail to make this a mandate. At the GM of old, Cohan said, managers got promoted by toeing the CEO's line and ignoring those external changes. "What looked ill-advised from the perspective of the customer and competitors was smart for those bucking for promotions."

This is not just a matter of employees sucking up to their higher-ups. One of the reasons for this aversion to listening to customer trends and feedback is the fundamental human tendency to filter out information that does not match up with our preconceived notions, which psychological researchers call the *confirmation bias*. This leads many of us to genuinely think that our products or services are superior when we should be open-minded about our limitations.

One of the most effective ways of overcoming this bias—to be sure you are aware of and open to problems and opportunities—is to create a culture of rigorous customer focus with channels for all employees to report upward issues that they are seeing on the front lines. In fact, the most profitable cultures we have studied not only listen for customer feedback but can be described as *active* in soliciting both the good and the bad—and consider seriously even some comments or criticisms that may seem off-the-wall at the time. As we're sure you have witnessed, in most companies negative customer feedback is hidden from view. And feedback that could lead to new directions all too often is ignored. Employees who do bring complaints or new customer leanings to the attention of senior leadership are often viewed with suspicion or, our favorite, blamed for creating the problems themselves. One sales director told us during a culture assessment at a manufacturing firm, "Two months after I came on board I told one of our executive team members that my customers were asking for lower-price, off-the-shelf products. They thought the stuff we were peddling was just too complex and expensive. I thought it made sense; I mean, who wouldn't want to pay less for something that does about the same job? She [the senior executive] told me, 'You're new. You don't get it yet. They are just trying to squeeze a better price out of you.' I didn't bring our product mix up again."

This senior leader had no desire to get into a strategy debate that would be tainted by one or two unhappy customer complaints. Her young sales director just hadn't caught the vision yet; customers wanted what they sold, he just had to convince them that the prices were worth it. In reality, this company's complicated, high-price solutions were going the way of the dodo, but leaders had been discounting the trend toward commoditization for a long time. They were too busy and too stressed to consider feedback like that, and, after all, things weren't *that* bad. Sure they had challenges, but who doesn't? It wasn't like they were about to shut the doors. Sales that quarter were up 4 percent!

What you don't know can and will hurt you. Research firm TARP has found that for every customer who complains, there are twenty-five who do not. That means if ten customers gripe about your service or products or pricing in a month, there may be another two hundred and fifty who just quietly dump you, never to call again.

Now, please don't misconstrue this chapter as just a guide to identifying early indications of problems with your products and services. It's also not about keeping up with the Joneses (your competitors), spotting new opportunities, or the obvious benefit of increasing customer satisfaction and repeat business. Those things are all important, we're sure you would agree, but our argument is not tactical; it's cultural. Your organization must evolve into one that not only rewards employees who spot customer trends or problems, but one that finds such challenges invigorating, one that empowers people at all levels to respond with alacrity and creativity.

After all, if a company isn't interested in acting upon negative customer feedback or giving employees the autonomy to do something positive to fix an issue, then the inevitable negative feedback every company gets from time to time is dispiriting and can leave people throughout the organization frustrated and resentful—undermining their commitment to the company's mission. Cultures that help their workers become sure-footed about making moment-to-moment judgment calls in dealing with issues are rare. These organizations create channels for employees to share feedback and they reward and publicize those who take positive risks. These are the firms that inspire their people to push the envelope to find great ideas, rather than just follow procedures.

Here are two contrasting examples. The first is personal: We called our business bank recently to ask for a letter of reference for a vendor. The woman who answered the phone at this nationwide bank was polite but said we'd need to come into the branch for the letter; that was policy. "But we are traveling and the letter is urgent," we argued. Sorry, there was nothing she could do. Ugh.

Contrast that with the example of Lisa DiStasio, assistant manager at the Clinton Shoreline, Connecticut, branch of First Niagara Bank. In an interview with us, DiStasio said, "A customer called me and didn't know where to turn. She was in Maine visiting her son and had hit a moose with her car. She didn't have the cash needed to make repairs and didn't know how to get money from her account here. I make it a point to get to know my customers, so they have someone to turn to when they need assistance. I recalled that First Niagara could accept a faxed wire request up to a certain amount. It would not be simple: Over the next couple of hours I worked with her by way of phone calls, e-mail, and fax to get the wire initiated and sent to her son's account. She was so relieved."

After the customer returned from Maine she brought DiStasio a flower arrangement. The woman told the entire staff that the assistance provided was above and beyond. Said DiStasio, "The thank-you surprised me because it is my responsibility to provide world-class service and do whatever I can to assist customers. The best part of my day is when I can make things better for a customer."

What a difference. From an environment where employees' hands are tied, to a place where employees feel they are expected to solve problems. What could be more engaging, enabling, and energizing than being trusted to solve issues such as this for your customers? (And in case you are wondering, no, we did not take flowers to our bank.)

Over the years we've met many managers who gave us keen insights about the value of being customer-focused. One of the more astute of those leaders is Mark Servodidio, chief administrative officer and executive vice president of Avis Budget Group, the 28,000-employee rental car business. When we visited Servodidio in his office in Parsippany, New Jersey, he suggested that the corporate world is divided into two basic types of organizations. The first is rules-based. They require customers and employees to fit into a rigid system, and leaders at these companies tend to think it's the rules that make them successful. Think of a typical fast-food chain. Any franchise in the chain can take sixteen-year-old Melissa; teach her how to make a burger, pizza, or taco; and within a few days she's a productive member of the restaurant. As a customer, you can order your burger without pickles, but you can't order a filet mignon. That kind of simplicity means that even if Melissa suddenly leaves for college, the restaurant will go on without her.

Rules-based companies can go along fine for quite some time, but most rarely experience breakthrough growth or innovation. There is no question that good processes are important, but making employees slaves to rules is no way to encourage ingenuity among them and seriously limits your ability to be nimble and respond to the ever-changing market we face today. As for customers, companies that adhere mindlessly to rules not only become annoying to deal with but are rarely considered partners that can solve our most pressing problems.

The other type of company Servodidio highlights truly heeds the voice of its customer. It actively seeks feedback not only from inside but from clients and suppliers. But how?

≈ ALL IN ≈

EIGHT WAYS TO DEVELOP
A CUSTOMER FOCUS

To begin your own process of instilling your people with a customer focus, ask yourself a few questions about your company: Are you primarily rules-based? Do leaders think it's the policies and processes that make you successful? Do your customers think you are hard to do business with because of all your rules? Are your frontline, customer-facing employees dealing with a fair amount of customer complaints? Do you know of high performers who have suggested better ways to serve client needs but who have been shot down? Are your people pointing out effective things your competitors are doing or bumps coming down the road, only to be ignored? How receptive overall are you to input from outside?

The answers should give you a good basic idea of how customer-focused you are. But then, what to do? What follows are eight key things you can do to get started on the process of focusing on your customers:

1. Give them more face time. The best way to gauge what customers are thinking is through back-and-forth communication either in person or on the phone, not via e-mail, and not just through impersonal surveys. If a customer offers a suggestion, restate it in your own words and repeat it back to ensure you understood correctly, and then write it down.

2. Prioritize requests. Some customers will have little to ask of you, and some will have a bevy of requests. That's fine, but ask these needy souls to order their suggestions by importance. Often a list of twenty suggestions yields only one or two deal-breakers. List their needs one through twenty, and do not allow multiple priority-one line items.

3. Thank them. Most people don't bother sending comments to merchants because they've been conditioned that such things go unnoticed. Let your customers know how much you appreciate their feedback by sending them a thank-you note, gift basket, or discount to your services. In addition, give them the best thanks of all: Update them with honest feedback about whether or not the change they suggested was possible to make and what your team has been doing about it.

4. Listen on social media. Facebook, Twitter, LinkedIn, etc. are "listening platforms," a great term coined by Dave Frankland of Forrester Research. Social media outlets make it easier than ever to listen to customers' concerns, see what makes them happy, and catch any problems immediately.

5. Listen to your front line. Employees receive the most regular evaluations from customers they serve every day, so ignore your frontline workers and especially your salespeople at your peril. Teach them active listening skills, and help employees strive to understand and document in detail what customers value and what they can do to deliver it better. Over time, companies use this data to make process and policy refinements that add up to a better experience for everyone.

6. Track trends. We often recommend our clients use a methodology like the Net Promoter score to do a regular check-up on the number of happy and unhappy customers. While this measurement has its detractors and shouldn't be the only tool you use long-term, it does give you a quick on-the-spot report card on how you're doing.

7. Create a customer forum. Create an online place where customers can connect with each other and with you. Treat the clients who provide feedback in this way as super-VIPs, and listen closely to what they have to say. Also, bring customers together in person on a customer advisory board. Handpick a dozen clients who not only get where you are trying to go but will give it to you straight if you are falling short.

8. Bring them to you. At your next employee meeting, host a customer panel featuring two or three key clients talking about what they like about your company, what makes them frustrated, and what the competitors are saying to lure them away. It will be one employee meeting where no one tunes out.

We saw this last idea firsthand in late 2011 when we were asked to address the Worldwide Procurement team at Johnson & Johnson. To close the conference, procurement leaders asked a customer to speak for a few minutes. She explained how a medicine made by a Johnson & Johnson company successfully treated her father's cancer—which was thought to be terminal. In an emotional address to the procurement team, she offered her family's thanks for their helping to ensure that vital medicines are accessible to the patients who need them. At the close of the conference, this one customer's story made very real the role these professionals have, and the impact they have on patients and their families. Good companies will tell you *what* they do and *how* they do it; great companies focus on *why* they do what they do for their customers.

≈ ALL IN ≈

SHHH. JUST LISTEN.

Becoming truly customer-focused can give your company a startling boost. As an example, we offer the new customer-focus initiative at global health insurance company Cigna, spearheaded three years ago by Ingrid Lindberg. As the chief customer experience officer, Lindberg came into an environment that was certainly competent and caring. In fact, 10 percent of Cigna's 30,000-person workforce are clinicians—nurses, behavioral health specialists, substance abuse experts, and so on—who work to influence the well-being and health of employees (whom they call *customers*) in the companies they serve (what they call their *clients*). The job of these clinicians is to reach out to people at risk—smokers, heavy drinkers, those with uncontrolled health issues—to suggest programs that could save their lives and reduce health care costs. What does all that mean? Let's say your cholesterol is high and you have Cigna as an insurance company. There's a good chance that after your doctor's visit one of these nice folks will give you a call to discuss your options and make some recommendations on how you might take better care of yourself.

It's all admirable, but Lindberg asked two important questions on her first few days on the job: "Is this what our clients want from us?" and second, "If they do want it, do customers trust us enough to accept the advice?"

Lindberg started talking with clients and customers and listening to their concerns. She even typed "Cigna sucks" into a few search engines and Twitter and then talked online to those who wrote the comments. The customers were shocked that they were talking to a real person who cared. She says, "They overwhelmingly told us, 'We want you to be easier to do business with and more understandable. Period. After you do these things, then you can tell me that my cholesterol is high, and I'll listen to you and trust you.'"

Hard to do business with and hard to understand—it probably sounds like an insurance company you've dealt with in the past. Lindberg was on a mission to fix that, and she started with the touch point where customers most often come into contact with their insurance company: the explanation of benefits, or EOB. That's the form your insurance company sends to you after every doctor's visit, explaining what medical treatments and services will be paid for.

"We asked how we could improve our EOB," she says. "Customers had no idea what we were talking about. Some said, 'Do you mean the "This Is Not a Bill" form?'" Yep, that's the one. Like most insurance companies, Cigna had those five words emblazoned in twenty-four-point capital letters at the top of every page, as if that was the most important information their customers needed to know. The language they were using just wasn't helping real families.

So Lindberg put through a mandate at the highest level. She instituted a policy, still in force today, that requires Cigna's most senior executives to listen to one hour of live customer calls every week and then write a report on what they've heard. "They need to know how complex our business is for our customers," she says.

And that listening drove compassion. Not only has Cigna rewritten all its forms and documents into plain English (winning just about every award possible in the insurance industry), they also became the first major health insurer to offer live phone support twenty-four hours a day, seven days a week. That kind of coverage wasn't popular with a few inside the company, but clients and customers gratefully accepted it.

"When your toddler gets sick and you need to know where to take her for care, it's usually not at three P.M. but at three A.M.," Lindberg says. "So customers appreciate it. And clients love it because their people aren't making insurance calls during work hours."

Lindberg jokes that in the past Cigna phone lines had an automated response in the middle of the night that said, "We are open eight A.M. to five P.M., Monday through Friday. We are here to help, just not now."

During one of our interviews, she said that the night before a call had come in to a customer service representative in the middle of the night. "The rep was taking calls in her fuzzy pink slippers and a woman called who was acting irrationally. Finally the customer hung up. The rep called a nurse on duty, a behavioralist, and she agreed there could be a problem. They tried to call the customer back but got no answer, so they called the police. When the authorities arrived they found the woman had swallowed a bottle of pills and downed a pint of alcohol. She would most likely have died if we weren't answering phones at three A.M.

"We hear a story like this every week."

As a result of this renewed focus on customer needs, the insurer is not only saving lives but has seen an amazing 80 percent increase in people saying, "Cigna values me as a customer," and a 50 percent rise in customers agreeing with the statement "Cigna has my best interests at heart." In addition, customer trust scores have increased, helping Cigna truly deliver on its goal of improving health and wellness in all its more than sixty-six million customer relationships worldwide.

Oh, and one last note. Cigna in 2010 increased revenues by 15 percent to $21.3 billion.

Isn't it amazing what can happen when you really listen to your customers and ensure everyone in the organization is attentive to their needs?

≈ ALL IN ≈

WHO IS YOUR CUSTOMER?

By this point, many managers might be arguing that their culture *is* customer-focused already. For instance, if you worked in health care and we asked, "Who is your customer?" you'd answer, "The person lying in the hospital bed." Right? Well, that wasn't the answer one hospital received when they asked their employees that question and really listened to the answers.

Four and a half years ago, when Shane Spees took over as president and CEO of the 4,300-employee Baptist Health System in Alabama, he discovered something surprising. "Most employees thought our customers were our *doctors*. Employees wanted to please the physicians first, not the patients."

It was a wake-up call for any health system that wants to value customer satisfaction. What hospital doesn't? And it begs the question: How off target are your employees about their priorities? How off target is your customer focus?

In the mid-2000s, Baptist Health System leaders began implementing a change process to institute a laserlike focus on the people they served and how they served them in order to make the company truly customer-focused, and this process was instrumental in bringing about a larger transformation of the company's culture. Four years ago the hospital system suffered from low employee morale, low retention, poor physician satisfaction, and lower-than-average patient quality scores. Today, the system reports 89 percent of its patient quality measures are in the top 10 percent of all hospitals in the United States, which means it can *prove* it has an extremely strong customer focus. And in 2010 the system ranked in the top fifteen places to work in Alabama, showing it has made great strides in its employee engagement and satisfaction too.

Spees and his leadership team began this transition with a question: How do we provide such an outstanding level of service to our patients that they actually become loyal to our hospitals, so that a person will want to come back to Baptist Health System if they need care in the future?

Unlike many leaders, Spees didn't think he had all the answers. The new CEO spent his first ninety days on the job just listening to employees, managers, physicians, and customers. The company had articulated that being "compassionate to customers" and "advocating for what is best for patients" were core values, but most employees had little idea just how exactly they were supposed to follow through on those customer-oriented values on a daily basis, moment to moment, whether in admitting patients to the emergency department or drawing blood for the lab.

So through employee focus groups, leaders defined each of the core values for people throughout the system. Today, no matter what position you hold, you have several examples of what integrity looks like on the job and what compassion means to customers. What many of us overlook in business is that values should be defined for the person at the bedside or working the front counter or answering phones, not just for senior leaders.

At Baptist Health, all of this has helped the company transform its culture from one of confusion to one of clarity.

"Never underestimate the power of your culture," Spees says. "It takes discipline as an organization to create engagement. We need staff and physicians to understand how their jobs relate to the goals and objectives of the organization. We need managers to coach and train employees and hold them accountable. And we need to remember it's not just about making sure people get results, it's about recognizing them when you see them doing it—that's what makes a culture great." In fact, Spees ends every one of his meetings with managers with a quote from leadership guru Peter Drucker: "Culture eats strategy for breakfast." He wants leaders at all levels throughout the system to understand that their health services can be replicated, but what can't be copied is the quality of the service of their people.

That customer-focus-driven culture transformation has helped Baptist Health System's transition over the past four years—to the tune of a $25 million annual improvement in profits (getting the system out of the red).

One last example of a company that you would expect to be rules-based but where a customer focus has won out is Chick-fil-A. When a new restaurant opens, owner/operators go out of their way to be creative in making raving fans in the area. If you see a new Chick-fil-A going up in your neighborhood, here's an inside tip: Many of those who stop by the construction site will get invited to a free dinner the night before the official opening. And those who show up for the special dinner also get ten coupons for free meals and are deputized as Chick-fil-A ambassadors. They promise to spread the word and hand out each coupon to a different person, someone unfamiliar with one of the tastiest chicken sandwiches on the planet.

"One thing we've learned," said Senior Vice President Tim Tassopoulos, "is when a customer says to a friend, 'Come eat with me at Chick-fil-A,' there is no higher recommendation."

President and COO Dan Cathy wants his owner/operators to "stretch the tent," to create an environment where everyone feels welcomed as part of the Chick-fil-A family, not just those owners and team members, but their families and the communities around them.

And if you don't have a Chick-fil-A location near you, it might be on purpose. The Cathy family has chosen to limit growth to keep customer satisfaction high. Says Tassopoulos, "In the restaurant business, you are only as good as the last meal. So we want to do things right, every time, every day. As we expand, we build businesses that can deliver on the Chick-fil-A experience that customers have come to trust."

≈ ALL IN ≈

WHO ARE YOUR VISIONARIES?

The idea of a customer focus means not only becoming more responsive to client desires in the day-to-day processes of your business, but implementing methods of working with customers that dramatically change the way you do things. This obviously requires leadership to put more responsibility in the hands of certain key employees. And while many leaders think they have all the answers, most C-suites typically don't have the specific operational knowledge or the time to critique all the ways the business is operating and draft new ways forward. And clearly you can't have the whole company involved to the same degree in redesigning processes.

In the most innovative cultures we've studied, leaders have taken select numbers of enterprising employees out of their normal jobs for a time and asked them to push the entire organization forward. These top performers are given permission to disrupt and innovate with the customer in mind.

While rules-based companies tend to operate according to the principle that everyone at the various levels and in the various functions adds value about equally, the fact is there are employees at all levels who are higher performers, and it's these people who are often the most connected to your customers—they have learned how to provide valued service and they will bring the most creativity and innovative thinking to driving a customer-enhancement process.

At Avis Budget Group, leaders have undertaken such a course. As Mark Servodidio sees things, "customer-based organizations value their people above their processes. They focus on the voice of the customer and they organize their best talent around those customer needs." As such, Avis Budget Group has assembled a cross-functional team with some of the company's most talented employees, directed by a former HR person, and including a salesperson, two operations people, a finance person, and an IT person. They are high-potential leaders who have been pulled out of their jobs to address customer issues.

Says Servodidio, "They are attacking one by one what our clients call our pain points—whether issues with our invoices or the return process or the website or customer service center. They've got the talent to think about organizational capability and change, to think about technology and how it works in the operation, and they've been given permission to challenge and then come back and work with the functions to move the needle significantly to meet the customer need, as opposed to each function doing their own thing."

Avis asks these people to think for themselves in analyzing the ways the company can make improvements, and in recognition of the quality of their contribution it incents and pays them differently and measures their performance in a unique manner. Leadership has come to realize that while systems and rules make the company reliable and consistent, it's tapping into the talents of people like this—asking them to take more responsibility for really interacting with customers and formulating strategies—that will drive innovation and breakout results.

We are big fans of teamwork. We've written a book about the subject and help organizations around the world build more cooperative environments. And yet we also understand the power of putting certain special individuals on the case in this way to change an organization for the better. In late 2011, Facebook CEO Mark Zuckerberg made a comment to *The New York Times* on the ever-escalating war for talent in Silicon Valley. He had just paid $47 million to acquire FriendFeed, a price that translated to about $4 million per employee. His point has a ring of truth to it, even if his math might be a bit off: "Someone who is exceptional in their role is not just a little better than someone who is pretty good. They are 100 times better." Marc Andreessen, the cofounder of Netscape and now one of Silicon Valley's most high-profile venture capitalists, added this: "The gap between what a highly productive person can do and what an average person can do is getting bigger and bigger. Five great programmers can completely outperform 1,000 mediocre programmers."

These might be mathematical exaggerations, but we've often seen the larger truth of what they're saying. Take the sales organization we worked with where the average rep closed about 20 percent of their deals in competitive situations. Sales rep Ana's close rate was 60 percent. Was she a hundred times better than the mediocre reps? No. But she was quantifiably three times better, and that equated to hundreds of thousands of dollars more in the bank every year in her region. The question to pose seemed obvious to us: *Why don't you rewrite Ana's job description so she's involved with every big deal?* The answer: It was political.

There are outstanding people like Ana in every department, performers who if allowed could make a significant difference for your customers. The question is, do you trust your best people to push and innovate in meeting client demands? Are you open to giving talented people more latitude to challenge the status quo in this way and develop a true customer focus?

Step Summary

CREATE A CUSTOMER FOCUS
ARE YOU LISTENING?

- Most organizations are oblivious to what customers find attractive about rivals. The best leaders encourage vigilance for disruptive solutions or trends that might harm or benefit their firm.
- A culture of customer focus provides channels for employees to report upward issues they see on the front lines, rewards them when they spot something important, encourages them to find challenges invigorating, and empowers people at all levels to respond to those challenges with alacrity and creativity.
- Successful companies can fall into various traps: physical, in which current investments prevent the pursuit of something new; strategic, failing to anticipate the future; and psychological, fixating on what made them successful and failing to notice something new displacing it.
- Rules-based companies discourage ingenuity among employees and seriously limit their ability to respond to an ever-changing market.
- Customer-focused organizations actively seek feedback from clients.
- In customer-focused firms, leadership puts more responsibility in the hands of key employees who are asked to push the entire organization forward. They are given permission to disrupt and innovate with the customer in mind.
- Ask yourself: Do you trust your best people to push and innovate in meeting customer demands? Are you open to giving talented people more latitude to challenge the status quo in this way?

6

Develop Agility

Helping Employees Deal with Change

Just after midnight on April 12, 1961, Yuri Gagarin left his apartment and took a short bus ride to the Baikonur Cosmodrome, a hastily erected collection of tin-sided buildings nestled in the desert steppes of Kazakhstan. He ate a quick breakfast and then climbed into a silver space suit, covered it with a set of garish orange overalls, and then stuffed his diminutive five-foot-two-inch frame into a cockpit barely larger than a steamer trunk and the shape of a cannonball.

What happened next has become a proud part of Russian history, a tale told to every schoolchild in that country. For ninety minutes, Soviet cosmonaut Gagarin waited anxiously in the metal capsule atop the 125-foot *Vostok* rocket, a retrofitted missile that had been designed to launch nuclear explosives. He had only his nerves to keep him company. At one point he joked into his headset, "Is my heart still beating?" The answer was grave from the Russian scientists on the other end: "Pulse sixty-four." "Oh, good," he responded, deadpan, "so my heart *is* beating."

Finally, at 9:07 A.M. local time, the all-clear was given and four booster rockets ignited. The earth shook as the *Vostok* lifted off the ground—climbing slowly at first but then faster and faster until the primitive rocket reached the speed of a bullet, 17,000 miles an hour. Two minutes later, looking through a porthole in the front of the cockpit, Yuri Gagarin saw the sky change from blue to gray, and then to black, as he became the first human to break out of Earth's atmosphere. Oceans and continents spun past, but inside the capsule Gagarin chuckled as a pencil floated by him in the zero-gravity environment. He was in space.

The entire mission had been conducted in great secrecy. Even Gagarin's wife was unaware of the operation. Soviet officials had decided that no one need ever know if the cosmonaut didn't survive the immense pressure of the launch. They didn't have to worry. Just minutes after liftoff, when it was clear that Gagarin was healthy, radio broadcasters began announcing that the USSR had successfully launched a man into orbit. The news sent thousands cheering into the streets of Moscow.

Leap ahead to the end of his mission. Gagarin's parachute floated him back to earth near the Russian town of Saratov, ironically not far from where he took his first flight as a young pilot. There, the handsome twenty-seven-year-old son of a carpenter and a farm laborer instantly became a national hero.

In the days that followed, the excitement would turn into a frenzy. Indeed, Gagarin's 108-minute circumnavigation of the globe would become the story everyone worldwide wanted to hear. Almost immediately Gagarin was sent on a public-relations tour of Italy, England, Canada, and Japan to promote the achievement. Communist Party officials knew precisely what they were doing: They were rubbing it in. They had beaten the United States in the race to space. Three weeks later, on May 5, Alan Shepard would go into orbit too, but even then the American would only fly a short, suborbital flight instead of circling Earth as Gagarin had done just a few weeks before.

It was a great embarrassment for the United States, which viewed itself as a superior superpower, but having been bested by the Soviets was especially irksome for President John F. Kennedy. The tall, slender Bostonian was a man of great resolve and intelligence, but more than anything, he just hated to lose. Eunice Kennedy Shriver remembered that as a boy her brother would become awfully cross if he lost a simple game of checkers, and he would insist on playing again and again until he had won more times than his opponent.

It was with this indefatigable spirit that the president, on May 25, 1961, addressed a special joint session of Congress. He outlined the dramatic and ambitious goal of sending an American safely to the moon. He explained that it would be a challenging technological feat. To make it, they would have to invent materials and technologies that didn't exist at the time. But, he explained, the race for the moon was the next big area of exploration for mankind, and it was a race where the U.S. actually had a lead on the Soviets.

"Space is open to us now," said Kennedy. "I believe that this nation should commit itself to achieving the goal, before this decade is out, of landing a man on the moon and returning him safely to the earth. In a very real sense, it will not be one man going to the moon—if we make this judgment affirmatively, it will be an entire nation. For all of us must work to put him there."

Indeed, that notion, "all of us must work to put him there," was more than apt. Only the construction of the Panama Canal and the Manhattan Project would be comparable in scope to what the president was asking of his country of "free men." NASA's overall human spaceflight efforts would involve the work of tens of thousands of scientists and technicians, as well as the support and funding of the entire country. All would be guided by Kennedy's vision, which extended from that single speech to a series of public challenges to his people to "be bold" and reach the moon before the decade was over. He was frank about the financial obstacles and technical challenges, and he laid them out as a shared burden. In 1962, he said that space program expenditures would rise to fifty cents per week for every man, woman, and child in the country.

Kennedy's words remain to this day *the* definitive speech on change management.

And they struck a chord. While NASA was struggling to keep up with Gagarin's historic flight, Kennedy—using just words— put America in the position of front-runner. When you think about it, the notion was actually outlandish—that America could set foot on the moon so quickly with little track record to predict its success. To safely land a man on an orbiting chunk of rock some 240,000 miles from our planet would be an astounding triumph considering the difficulty and all the things that weren't known. After all, it had never been done before—by anyone. No one had even come close. Yet few in the U.S. scoffed at the idea. It quickly became the nation's shared belief. Financial backing was attained almost without resistance to build the gigantic Manned Spacecraft Center near Houston and initiate Project Gemini. And on July 20, 1969, a mere eight years after Kennedy's first rallying speech, the vision of a mission to the moon became history when *Apollo 11* commander Neil Armstrong stepped off the lunar module's ladder and onto the moon's dusty surface.

So was it outlandish? Not at all, because an entire nation became *agile*.

Transformation occurs when a leader anticipates change and helps us embrace it. New worlds are discovered, governments are built, laws are written, religious and civic organizations grow, communities bond, and corporate cultures thrive when our leaders see potential on the horizon and help us adapt.

This chapter is about that kind of remarkable vision in leaders and how it contributes to a culture of belief. It's about how some managers are able to help their people feel confident about facing the future or facing a shared fear.

≈ ALL IN ≈

MANAGING CHANGE: THE EVIDENCE

When we initiated the research that formed the basis for this book, we certainly didn't foresee the concept of agility arising as one of the top skills of leaders in high-performance organizations. After all, in his business classic *Good to Great*, Jim Collins wrote, "Great companies paid scant attention to managing change." He believed that under the right conditions the problems of change largely melt away. That may have been true when

Collins's book was released in 2001; today it is no longer so. And perhaps it shouldn't have been true back then. All one needs to do is look at the example of Circuit City to appreciate that organizations should be extremely attentive to the shifting world around them. The retailer had the highest fifteen-year stock market return of any of the *Good to Great* companies, and yet it liquidated its last U.S. store in 2009. From great to gone in a decade.

The new data shows that there is no doubt that today, in this floundering economy, high-performance managers are vastly more agile at helping guide employees through the vagaries of the marketplace—and that can lead to stunning financial results.

Here's some more recent evidence. When Towers Watson's researchers took a deeper dive into their Global High Performance group database, looking at just 2010 data, they found thirteen of the high-performance companies were more effective at "managing change" than their peers. Remember, the other high-performance firms were still very profitable in their own right but were less able to respond to challenges from competitors and other market forces. Now, here's the crux of the finding: The thirteen "change masters" reported three-year revenue growth a whopping three times higher than their high-performance peers.

So what was different about the culture in these most agile of places? First, change started with managers who were considered "authentic" by their people. That meant leaders at all levels provided a clear sense of direction and made decisions promptly, they treated employees respectfully and took action on issues their people raised, and finally they behaved in alignment with company values.

To sum it up, they got off the dime and truly walked the talk.

Second, on an organizational level, these agile companies faced competitive market pressures head-on through innovative product development, a customer-focused culture, and social responsibility and integrity in dealing with their clients.

In short, employees felt they could trust their leaders to make the company better, all while doing the right thing for customers.

And third, managers used sophisticated talent-management

practices to attract, develop, promote, and retain the best people; they ensured employees had regular, clear, and objective performance evaluations; and they fairly recognized efforts through nonmonetary measures.

We would put it succinctly by saying this: In the most agile companies, maybe leaders were actually listening to HR. Who would have thought it?

At any rate, we see that agility is more important in sustaining above-average business results than clever strategy, compelling product mix, or the other typical focuses of leaders. Yet think about the time-tested list of prized management skills that are usually touted: knowledge, dependability, courage, vision, fairness, optimism, collaboration, composure, fun. Agility rarely shows up on such lists . . . and to be honest, it hasn't appeared on our leadership surveys either—that is, until now. It is emerging because of the quickening pace of change in business that's come with new technology and globalization, as well as the pressures of the recent economic downturn. Today, employees feel a heightened need for their leaders to help them adapt. One interviewee we met with put this very clearly: "I have my head down doing my work. We're going two hundred miles an hour here. I need my leaders to be looking to the horizon."

Without a leader's realistic and yet inspirational vision of the future, there can be no dream of what can be. Dr. Martin Luther King Jr. didn't gather his followers and say, "I'm not sure what the future holds, but come with me anyway." Nor did he use the practical yet uninspiring words "I have a plan." Instead King laid out a clear, stirring vision of a future and said, "I have a dream," and a nation developed the agility necessary to see that it would become reality.

But what exactly do we mean by *agility* in terms of organizational impact? Agility is helping a team or an entire company evolve and meet the future in new and innovative ways. But it's important to note that organizational agility is different from flexibility. The first is active, the latter passive.

Flexibility is the ability of a work group to respond to changing circumstances. It's been around in business literature for decades. Agility, however, is a more recent addition to the business lexicon. Lehigh University researchers were among the first to study this subject, and we outline their findings briefly in the bullets below. In short, if we lined up high-performance cultures for review, you'd see these points of similarity in how they embrace change:

Enrichment. An agile company enriches the lives of its customers, often selling tailored solutions to meet specific problems. Take the personal computer industry, which has now reached near-commodity status. To avoid competing solely on price (rarely a good idea), companies are differentiating by allowing customers to custom-order machines that match their personal needs—with the speed, software, mobile access, and level of support they need.

Cooperation. An agile culture employs the "core competence" approach, which means it does what it's best at and then forms alliances to fulfill all noncore functions. As more than one senior leader has told us lately, "The future is about partnerships." Not everything has to be created or done in-house.

Organization. The most agile companies aren't afraid to allow different, interesting organizational structures to exist, reflecting the diversity of the tasks it has to perform to meet customer requirements. And in these firms, people and assets are redeployed and reconfigured rapidly when the market shifts.

Leverage. Finally, according to the Lehigh University study, the most agile organizations leverage the impact of people and information, with an emphasis on putting their talent and intelligence up against the most value-added products.

Perhaps no leader was more agile than Steve Jobs, at least not since Walt Disney or Henry Ford was around. While Jobs did not invent computer science, broadband, or recorded music and entertainment, he brought them to the masses with elegant, stylish, and above all user-friendly devices and packaging that demystified the technology.

Jobs's work with Apple is legendary, but equally extraordinary and less well known is his transformation of Pixar, which he purchased in 1986 (when the company was called the Graphics Group) from George Lucas for $5 million. Jobs led the company's evolution from a forty-person computer-graphics house into an animated movie company that has earned twenty-six Academy Awards and today puts out films with the highest average box office gross of any studio in the industry.

How did he do it? He didn't waste time trash-talking his opponents. He simply encouraged his teams to do things better and was well known for rolling up his sleeves and helping his people assess what was working and what wasn't. As Jobs said, "Sometimes when you innovate, you make mistakes. It is best to admit them quickly, and get on with improving your other innovations."

≈ ALL IN ≈

WHY IT HURTS

So why don't more leaders do this? Why don't more leaders help their employees navigate the uncertainties of their turbulent markets? For one thing, because change hurts. That's not metaphorical. According to experts at the University of Pennsylvania Behavioral Health Corporate Services, change at work induces a physiological reaction in employees that automatically increases blood pressure, heart rate, respiration, metabolism, and blood flow to muscles. This stress response in nature is intended to help your body react quickly and effectively to any high-pressure situation. And yet over time, as you can imagine, the reaction on the job leads to stress and discomfort.

It's not in our nature to seek out such pain in the office; it's not even in our nature when it might save our lives. Consider this: In numerous studies of patients who have undergone coronary bypass surgery, on average only one in nine people adopts healthier day-to-day habits. As you can see, this resistance to change is a strong biological force, and it certainly isn't a habit of most managers to help us deal with it.

But to achieve an agile culture, leaders must confront human nature and help alter it. According to Jeffrey M. Schwartz, a UCLA research psychiatrist, and David Rock, co-creator of the management coaching curriculum at New York University, leaders of high-performing teams focus employee attention away from the pain naturally associated with change using experiences and language that point them toward rewarding insights and ideas about the new direction.

They offer a great example: "Two individuals working on the same customer service telephone line could hold different mental maps of the same customers. The first, seeing customers only as troubled children, would hear only complaints that needed to be allayed; the second, seeing them as busy but intelligent professionals, would hear valuable suggestions for improving a product or service."

How to help that first agent to see things differently? The researchers suggest one way is by cultivating moments of insight—creating experiences that will allow people to provoke themselves to change their attitudes and expectations more quickly and dramatically than they normally would. For instance, as simple starters, a leader might invite real customers into the work facility to speak with agents or could encourage agents to attend client meetings off-site. "The help-desk clerk who sees customers as children won't change the way he or she listens without a moment of insight in which his or her mental maps shift to seeing customers as experts," said Schwartz and Rock. "Leaders wanting to change the way people think or behave should learn to recognize, encourage, and deepen their team's insights." Creating in your organization a powerful expectation of change through these interpersonal awakenings can begin to counterbalance your people's normal physiological reactions.

Words and ideas from managers to their employees can also help provide a vocabulary of change that molds conversations and frames discussions in ways that help people to be receptive. On the flip side, agility is also aided by establishing processes for leaders to be constantly exposed to the upward insights of their employees. Workers are a font of information that leaders need. Few things are as valuable for a leader seeking to build his or her agility than to heed the advice of John Kotter of Harvard, who discovered that *effective* general managers spend more than 80 percent of their time interacting with others. Instead of hunkering down "getting their work done," by investing this time with employees, peers, and clients they were better able to perceive issues as they were arising and to gain the knowledge necessary to tackle those problems and formulate changes in strategy. Leaders must be open to ideas not only from those above them, but from peers and reports at all levels.

We term this unfiltered approach *360-degree listening,* and it can yield surprising results. Here's a charming example we found from a man named Brian in one of our focus groups in Seattle. He was an assistant restaurant manager with the responsibility of overseeing the dinner shift in a busy restaurant. In a staff meeting one evening he said he'd brought up a concern: Dinnerware breakage costs were killing them. After a fruitless discussion, the general consensus was that all of the recent dropped dishes and glasses had been accidents, and it was impossible to prevent mishaps by any "process improvement." Discouraged, Brian was about to move on to the next topic when the special-needs busboy, Israel, spoke up. "Too bad we don't have rubber floors."

"Everyone laughed, being nice—but then we realized he'd hit on the answer: rubber floor mats in the kitchen. Israel became the staff hero and our breakage is down like ninety percent," Brian told the focus group. "You never know where your next great idea will come from."

This is why a vital step in making sure your culture is agile is to encourage what we call "freeform communication," aiming for an open and robust exchange of employee ideas. This interchange is a fountain of creativity for agile work groups, helping all employees feel ownership and that they are an important part of the change process.

≈ ALL IN ≈

A HARD ROCK LESSON

Leadership from the top is important: Managers need to identify challenges and understand corporate direction, no doubt. But input, honest discussion, and ownership from your staff are powerful forces to move your organization forward.

Take the case of one restaurant chain that has experienced outstanding growth during a time when so many of its peers have either struggled or gone out of business. Hard Rock International has thrived while bucking conventional business thinking. When the first café opened in 1971 on Old Park Lane in London, one critic wrote that putting a burger-and-beer joint in the shadow of Buckingham Palace made about as much sense as serving sushi at Yankee Stadium. But Hard Rock tapped into a market ready to rebel against old-school snobbery. The eatery's "Love All, Serve All" motto anchored the upheaval, and Hard Rock has now spread worldwide with cafés, hotels, and casinos on six continents staffed by 20,000 employees providing what they irreverently call "kick-ass" service with a dash of rock and roll.

When the entire restaurant industry suffered after September 11, 2001, and just about every restaurant had a downturn, Hard Rock International didn't trim its staff. Instead, leadership let staff members know what was going on and then turned to them for ideas.

"Why not talk to your employees?" said Calum MacPherson, vice president of operations in Europe. "We told our people what we needed to work on, like we needed to find another fifty cents on each check, and they did it."

And the chain does this over and over. MacPherson added, "Helping our employees be agile is all about communication." And that begins every day before the restaurant even opens its doors. "The preshift meeting is huge. We need to get people fired up on a daily basis. And we tell them the truth. Here are the sales numbers from yesterday and what we hope to make today. Here's what we are good at and what we suck at. I love it when leaders couch things in business terms: We have areas of *opportunity*. That's bull—. You have weaknesses. We say, 'We've got to go fix this and we need your help.'"

All of this frankness and involvement in facing challenges has driven tangible results. During the worst decade in recent history for restaurants, Hard Rock grew consistently between 5 and 8 percent a year. But when the recession of 2008 hit, the chain asked employees to crank it up again and Hard Rock actually *tripled* that already impressive growth rate.

And in turn, Hard Rock pays employees back in unique ways for their agility, giving them a steady stream of recognition, a topic we'll explore in more detail later. For instance, every year in London's Hyde Park, Hard Rock puts on one of the largest rock shows in the world. They fly in employees from all over to set the park up. It's grueling work, sixteen-hour days for more than a week. And while the company throws gala events for VIPs and rock stars like Paul McCartney, Eric Clapton, and Stevie Wonder, the best party is reserved for after the show—and the only people invited are the staff.

"People know when you put on a crap party for them," MacPherson said. "We put on this amazing party for our people and we spend as much money on that as anything else we do that weekend. That's what people remember."

Of course, there is always a danger that such success will sabotage agility. The old metaphor rings true: It's harder to turn around a tanker than a tugboat. The larger you become, the more you are inclined to repeat the formula that brought you to this happy place—even when conditions change. How often have you heard, "That's not the way we do things around here," or some such phrase in your business life?

A company that has bucked this trend consistently is Rational AG, a German manufacturer of ovens for caterers. Following the trend we are recommending, they have done this in large part by instilling a culture of agility by incorporating employees into the process of looking out for necessary changes and rewarding innovation. The company's change vocabulary is clear in one of their core values: "Respecting our staff members and colleagues as emancipated people." We love that concept, the idea that their employees will give their best ideas if they are free from bondage, restraint, or paternal control. The firm asks managers to consider themselves not taskmasters but "gardeners" for their employees—helping people grow and evolve. As for employees, they are not only forewarned that processes and products need to improve to meet a market demand, they are actively asked to direct the solutions. This kind of agility has made Rational AG the market leader in thermal food preparation, with more than a 50 percent market share.

In this German firm, managers are trained to seek help for the smallest improvements, some of which have resulted in sizable productivity and quality gains. For instance, the assembly line is organized around customized order fulfillment, and parts for each thermal cooking unit are placed on carts, which are then transported to workstations for individual assembly. When employees were shown that competitors were catching up to their processes, they suggested installing wheels on these carts so they could be pushed by an employee instead of a forklift. Employees followed up by installing hook-and-eye hardware on those same carts so more than one could be moved at a time. Then an employee suggested that they raise the carts to waist level so assemblers were not bending down to retrieve parts. Upon implementation, Rational AG immediately experienced a gain in productivity—not to mention improving the work experience for their people.

≈ ALL IN ≈

360-DEGREE LISTENING

Brilliant ideas like that shouldn't be bottled up, but often they are. Why does it seem that we are asking leaders to pull out their own teeth when we encourage openness of communication and sharing of ideas between different branches, locations, or departments? How often do we visit a retail chain, for instance, where store managers in Seattle or Cincinnati do not communicate what's working because they feel as if they are competing with their fellow stores in Toronto or Dallas instead of the real competitors across the street? In organizations where freeform communication is not rewarded—where groups or individuals hoard their ideas—the direct consequence is increased waste and duplication.

Unable to find the information or knowledge they need, employees assume that it is not available, and so they re-create it or pay for someone to provide it, slowing the process of change. Most of us can relate to the frustration of the former CEO of HP when he lamented, "If HP only knew what HP knows."

Technology can be a powerful mechanism for facilitating this 360-degree listening—especially when controls from above are relaxed. Technology in and of itself does not necessarily increase agility, but we have visited numerous companies that use social networking portals on their intranets to encourage employees to exchange knowledge and innovative ideas. Some common forms of collaboration online include file sharing, wiki sites, blogging, and forums.

One of the best examples of this is found at venerable 115-year-old IBM, which encourages all of its 400,000 employees to share through internal online tools, driving collaboration and innovation. Employees can chat to each other or even blog to the public without corporate intervention. Said Adam Christensen, a member of the three-person social media communications department for the giant firm, "We don't police. The community's largely self-regulating. And that's worked wonderfully well."

That means about 100,000 of IBM's employees comment regularly on the 17,000 internal blogs, on every subject imaginable, from developing service-oriented architecture to sales best practices to parenting for the working professional.

"We're very much a knowledge-based company. It's really the expertise of the employee that we're hitting on," said Christensen. And the employee sharing tools are investments in making their people smarter and more nimble. It's a perfect example of what agility looks like at the grassroots level, where the best ideas usually grow.

Take a moment now to consider the three ideas we've presented so far in this seven-step section and how they build on one another and have a multiplying effect. Creating a customer focus, for example, contributes valuably to becoming more agile as well as giving clarity to each employee about the mission. Defining the burning platform helps employees accept the change needed for agility. The key to high-performance leadership is to utilize them together.

Okay, but can you learn these skills or improve them? Absolutely. We realize this might be getting a little uncomfortable, though, and an underlying reason is that building these skills requires you to suppress your natural levels of personal ambition and instead turn your focus toward others. Developing agility is square in that bull's-eye. The point is this: Quit worrying about yourself and lose yourself in helping those in your care. The results will be gratifying.

Next, we will explore a key way in which managers can build trust in their commitment to their people by developing transparency and sharing everything.

Step Summary

DEVELOP AGILITY
HELPING EMPLOYEES DEAL WITH CHANGE

- New data shows high-performance managers are vastly more agile at managing change and helping guide employees through the vagaries of the marketplace—which can lead to stunning financial results. The most agile companies in the Global High Performance database saw revenue growth three times higher than their high-performance peers.
- Agile managers provide a clear sense of direction and make decisions promptly, respectfully take action on issues raised by employees, and behave in alignment with company values.
- Agile organizations face competitive market pressures head-on through innovative product development, a customer-focused culture, and social responsibility and integrity in dealing with clients.
- Agile organizations also use sophisticated talent management practices to attract, develop, promote, and retain the best people; ensure employees have regular, clear, and objective performance evaluations; and fairly recognize high performers through nonmonetary measures.
- Additional research shows agile organizations *enrich* the lives of customers; *cooperate* using outside partners; *organize* in creative, responsive ways; and *leverage* their people and information to create value-added products.
- To help our employees change, we must cultivate moments of insight—experiences that allow people to provoke themselves to change their attitudes and expectations.
- As a manager, engage in 360-degree listening, encouraging input, honest discussion, and ownership from your staff and peers. Technology can be a powerful mechanism for facilitating this—especially when controls from above are relaxed.

7

Share Everything

Generating Trust
Through Transparent Communication

We were conducting a workshop in Atlanta in 2011 and asked participants a question designed to spur some debate: "What are you looking for in a great leader?" Among the responses of "vision," "communication," "honesty," and "fairness" came an answer we didn't expect: "I want my boss to make me a better person."

The man who said it wasn't looking for his business leader to change his core belief system—he was a devout Muslim, by the way. He wanted a boss who was an example, someone he could look up to, a person who challenged him to be even more trustworthy.

One of us once departed a company because our role models had left and there was no one remaining we trusted or wanted to emulate. Most likely you have felt that kind of void at one point in your career. You found yourself in a place where trust wasn't valued—perhaps a culture where information was shared only on a "need-to-know" basis, and you just never seemed to need to know anything.

When communication flows as feebly as an Arizona creek in July, it's either time to work to improve the culture or time to find a new place to work where people share everything.

The bottom line is this: Much of the distrust we see in work groups is a result of misunderstanding or misreading the intentions of others—especially leaders. When we aren't sure what's happening around us, we become distrustful. We are born that way. It's a reason children don't want to turn off the lights at bedtime. What are they afraid of? Not something they can see, but that something *unknown* is hiding in the closet.

In a dark work environment, where information is withheld or not communicated properly, employees tend to suspect the worst and rumors take the place of facts. It is openness that drives out the gray and helps employees regain trust in a culture. Through their example, leaders can create a contagion of openness that leads to trust and is a major contribution to a culture in which employees are engaged, enabled, and energized to give their all.

The powerful connection between open sharing and trust resonated when we discussed the idea with American Express vice president Doug DiPaola, who conducts quarterly "skip-level" meetings with the direct reports of his direct reports. In these meetings he not only shares everything he knows but asks the same from these employees. With no script or agenda, he starts each meeting with a series of probing questions. "I let them know I'm not there to get information to take back to their team leader or director," he says. "I really want a no-holds-barred conversation. And I explain, 'If you ask a question, you might not like it but I'm going to give you my honest response.'"

Catherine Cole, director of the American Express executive customer care group, also conducts skip-levels to enhance trust and openness. "I give these folks a forum to be able to share their ideas and concerns," says Cole. "I ask what can make their experience better. I meet with those people at least four times a year."

During Cole's skip-levels and town hall meetings, she is careful to document any concerns in an issue log. And over the ensuing weeks she follows up with the employees who raised those concerns to explain how they are being addressed. Our favorite idea from Cole for generating trust and openness was something she calls a Stay Interview. She gathers everyone who has a service anniversary during that month—whether for one year or thirty years of service—and asks them a series of great questions:

- Talk about your journey so far with American Express.
- Has your experience over the past year been beneficial to your growth and progress?
- What one or two things get you jazzed about coming to work every day?
- What makes you want to hit the snooze button?

Those last two questions are a fabulous way for Cole to understand the real concerns of her group, not to mention get this monthly anniversary group talking among themselves. And because her people know they work in a culture that isn't afraid to confront the brutal facts, and that their ideas and issues will be heard and logged by their director, employees share openly. Then, to add a touch of fun, at the end of the meeting Cole breaks out plastic champagne glasses, pours sparkling cider, and they all toast their service milestone.

It's important to note that leaders such as Cole and DiPaola aren't using such discussions with line employees as a pretense to have their people just *think* they have a voice; the conversations are part of a refreshing process designed to bring out the very best solutions, tied to a real goal on the part of the managers to share everything. It's just one way of many that leaders in this southern Florida American Express facility inspire open communication and trust, things that are harder and harder to gain in the turbulent financial marketplace.

"For the past three years it's been perpetual change," said Anne Marie Taglienti, the center's director of communications. "The economic collapse was a big wake-up call for our country and American Express was no exception. Leaders throughout the company have been honest about the situation. Doria [Camaraza] follows that commitment and informs us as soon as she knows something. It makes us all feel as if we are not just some call center somewhere, we are working to actually achieve something together, as a company."

As for Vice President Dean Vocaturo, he lives this step of sharing with his team by adherence to a set of rules such as "We communicate openly, honestly, and candidly," "We seek solutions and not blame," and "We try to involve people in decisions that affect them." Great sentiments, but he added that clear communication is number one. "I do town halls and go through the business results. I share the good, the bad, and the ugly. And the last couple years, credit losses and the regulatory environment have contributed to the challenges for our industry. But I also give hope. I tell them why this work is done in a proprietary operation versus a third-party outsourced call center. I explain how good we are in terms of timeliness, accuracy, and cost. And I tell them point-blank that's why it's important to reduce our operating expenses year after year."

While leaders often shy away from discussing hard truths—like the fact that many call centers have gone offshore—fearing they will dishearten their workers, there's something exhilarating about facing the facts head-on, something that helps people feel like they are being brought into the inner circle.

One honest conversation that stayed with us illustrated the fact that Senior Vice President Camaraza and her team weren't afraid to confront the hard reality of their market, and yet would only do it in an open, honest, and caring manner. During one of our meetings Camaraza was uncharacteristically late. When she swept in she apologized and explained she had to visit two employees whose jobs had been eliminated.

She said, "I went up to see these two people at their desks and thanked them on behalf of [CEO] Ken Chenault, the senior leadership team, and myself for their fifteen and twenty-four years of service. I asked them how they were doing and what place they were at emotionally. When I left, one of them said that the visit had meant more to him than anything that had happened. He actually said the whole process he'd been through had made him feel valued."

This kind of openness, especially about such delicate matters, is much too rare. So often in our travels we find organizations that are miserable at helping employees understand how well they are doing and whether or not they have a future within the organization, or at what level their opportunities may top out. At one manufacturing plant we toured, the HR manager had worked for twenty years to receive accreditations and certificates so he might take over when his vice president retired. When the day finally came to send in his application, he received a one-line e-mail response from an executive. It read, "We could not support you in this role." There was no interview. No face-to-face candor. Just twenty years of work and then those eight words that would shape his, his coworkers', and his family's perception of the company forever.

But in our interviews with the American Express Fort Lauderdale team, we were struck by how each member of the leadership team openly brought up painful issues without embarrassment. They seemed compelled to be brutally honest about the environment they were in, the changing workload, new government regulations. They were honest with employees about career opportunities and potential for growth. But despite the challenges of their work, each was passionately confident about their collective resilience. They would continue to win, they believed, especially if they learned from each other.

Camaraza has helped to drive openness and honesty, says DiPaola. "When Doria got here she challenged the way we looked at things. She wasn't afraid to be very overt about saying how things need to operate or how we need to work together as a team. She actively engaged each of us to drive toward a culture of excellence, to take ownership and accountability."

To achieve that kind of transparency, according to DiPaola, "people have to have a venue that is not just with their team leader, not just with their director, but with their leadership team member." He says, "I have a true open-door policy, and when I walk around the floor it's not a flyby. I've seen managers ask an employee, 'How are you?' And you hear, 'Oh, good,' before the employee has completed a sentence. It's like, 'Hihowareyougood.'"

And so DiPaola, this very busy vice president with hundreds of employees and intense customer pressures, takes time with each person. He learns about their families and their hobbies, and most important, he builds a tangible trust by sharing everything.

Vice President Steve Gaswirth summed it up well during our interview: "Communication is the key to everything. We listen and we explain. There are times we can incorporate employee suggestions into our strategy and there are times we can't. There are decisions made above us that we like, and some we might not agree with as a leadership team, but we always explain the reasoning."

≈ ALL IN ≈

TRUST ME

Ingrid Lindberg is a force of nature, a self-proclaimed triple-A personality who runs on too much caffeine. Early in her career Ingrid was, like many, trying to get ahead in the corporate world, working late. One night at ten thirty P.M. her boss at the time approached her desk. She says the exchange went like this:

Boss: Go home, Ingrid.
Ingrid: I will, I just have one more thing to do.
Boss: Ingrid, I don't want you to make this job your life. There's nothing that can't wait.
Ingrid: I know, I know.
Boss: Let me make this perfectly clear, Ingrid. I can replace you in twenty-four hours. That's the hard reality. Go home.

As we've told people Lindberg's story, a few gentle souls have gasped. After all, wasn't her boss telling her she could be replaced in a single day? How cruel. But Lindberg says, "I loved him for that. I learned to trust him because of that. He was looking out for me."

When the December holidays rolled around, Lindberg's boss approached her again. "Where are you going on vacation this year?" he asked.

"I thought I might take a week and visit my parents in Hawaii," she explained.

He shook his head. "This year you are going for two weeks. There's nothing here that can't wait a couple of weeks."

And the night before she left on that vacation, the boss insisted that she turn in her BlackBerry and laptop, explaining, "I know you. You'll work. This is your time to relax. We've got you covered. Remember, I can replace you in twenty-four hours."

For Lindberg, her relationship with her Twenty-four-Hour Manager translated everything in this conversation into a positive, because she had confidence in this man's principles and intentions. She knew that he wanted her rested and focused—because that was best for her and the company in the long run.

In contrast, you've probably worked for someone on the other end of the spectrum where you viewed their every move with suspicion. In our interviews for this book, we encountered many such instances of trust lost. An employee named Katrina told us one poignant story. Recognizing that their company had gradually sunk into a culture of avoidance—avoidance of accountability, avoidance of sharing, even avoidance of hard work—her leaders had committed publicly to building a more enthusiastic, open organization. She explained, "They [the executive team] started out in good faith by sending leaders to training sessions and getting them on board with the direction and the new language of the culture. Eventually these early adopter leaders would help to roll the concept out to the rest of the organization. It looked promising. But then things started to become, well, freaky."

Leaders who came back from training acted differently. They hugged each other in the halls. They were loud in meetings and organized ball-toss games in their offices with music blaring. Their cheery behavior clashed with the library-like atmosphere that had been the status quo of the firm for decades.

"The rest of us were still speaking in whispers in our cubes," said Katrina.

But worse, to preserve the integrity of the training for others who would experience it later, returning leaders were instructed not to discuss the training content. Employees outside the closed doors could only listen to their thunderous cheers—and make wild speculations.

"Leadership became a secret club," said Katrina. "The rest of us were not excited, we were suspicious." When leadership became aware of employee perceptions, they were shocked. How could something so purely positive in intention go so wrong?

What had colored the rollout? Was it the happy leaders bouncing balls in their offices (whatever *that* was about)? No, it was an underlying culture of mistrust. Employees had long-standing complaints about workload management, lack of honesty about the company's direction, and other issues, Katrina explained. "These hadn't been addressed and employees viewed management as unresponsive and uncaring. So when the top-down training was rolled out, instead of the secrecy building excitement and interest—an 'I can't wait until my turn' feeling—employees saw the changes as a threat and their exclusion as yet another insult."

People inevitably build a backstory for leadership decisions, and whether they trust you or not is the most significant determiner of whether that story will be positive or negative. Unfortunately, around the world, the trend seems to lean heavily toward the latter. For instance, in the United States, three out of four people don't believe there is any correlation between what campaigning politicians promise to do and what they will actually do if elected. Two out of three consumers don't trust even long-standing companies to make safe, durable products without the government setting industry standards (ironic, since they don't trust politicians). And 55 percent of people believe that companies will take advantage of the public if they think they can get away with it.

How about in the workplace? Only 36 percent of employees

believe their leaders operate with integrity and honesty. And the number one reason employees say they act unethically is because their boss models that behavior for them—often in subtle ways. Had enough bad news yet?

"Our work schedule is four ten-hour days and a three-day weekend," said one of our interviewees in a state government agency. "I get here before my boss in the morning every day and I stay after he leaves, every single day. I know he's not putting in forty hours, so when he gets up in staff meetings and preaches to us about acting ethically, I have to work really hard not to blatantly roll my eyes."

It's not an overstatement to say that trust transforms business relationships. Employees are drawn to trusted leaders, sometimes following them from organization to organization. A quote by George MacDonald comes to mind: "Few delights can equal the mere presence of one we trust utterly."

For a moment, imagine how your life would change if your significant other, children, extended family, neighbors, and friends did not trust you. Now consider what happens if one, two, or more of your employees, peers, or bosses don't trust you. The core question is this: Are you willing to become the person whom others will trust? We say "willing" because trust doesn't happen by accident. Trust is not a default setting in a relationship. Furthermore, all trust is not created equal. Real trust is the cornerstone of leadership, and it's thankfully a skill that you can improve. "Trust becomes an extension of who you are," said Stephen M. R. Covey, author of *The Speed of Trust*. Since we give more of our ideas and effort to leaders we trust and we are more apt to buy products from trustworthy companies, Covey argues that trust speeds up the pace of business. "It is a hard-edged economic driver. When trust goes up, speed goes up, and cost goes down. When trust goes down, speed goes down, and cost goes up."

And yet contrary to popular opinion, there's nothing simple about this subject. It's complicated, or at least the kind of leadership trust that can move a team forward is. On one level, society requires us to trust some people simply because of their role or position. For example, we implicitly have to trust our emergency room doctor, our airline pilot, the plumber who answers our midnight call, the computer repair tech, and even the kid operating the roller-coaster ride at the carnival. "Keep your arms and legs in the ride at all times," he mutters as he fastens you in (the wind whistling through his tongue ring).

We call this kind of trust *capability-based trust*. It means, "I trust your ability to solve a certain problem or help me at a certain point in time." It's generally short-term and situational, but it is an important first rung in the ladder of any business relationship. If we don't trust someone's capability, it's hard to move forward. For instance, doubts about the abilities of his senior leaders had been a rub for one employee we met. Marcus told us, "Our new CIO got his degree at a decidedly C-level business school and people just can't get over that. When he gets up in meetings and skims over a number, I can't help but wonder if he's purposely skirting it because it exposes a weakness. Our company is struggling, and I know it has to do with a lot of factors, but there's this idea out there among employees that leadership isn't fully qualified. It comes up more and more."

Capability-based trust such as that is foundational. Like food or shelter, people must first be confident their leader has the requisite knowledge, skills, experience, and even qualifications. And yet if those basics are in place—and let's face it, most of the time they are—we then look for something more in our leaders. We call it *character-based trust*. This is created over time by consistent behavior, adherence to principles, openness, honesty, and dependability. It grows as we watch how a leader acts in public and in private. It deepens as we judge someone's motives to be pure and nonthreatening and as we come to believe that our leader genuinely cares about his employees as individuals and demonstrates concern for our well-being and growth. This type of trust creates psychological safety in followers, which is the belief that our place on the team is safe for individual risk-taking, a place where we can give our all because someone in charge is looking out for us. And that leads to loyalty.

Without such character-based trust, many terrified soldiers would not follow their sergeants into a firefight. It's what allows employees to give their whole hearts and minds to an inspiring supervisor. You've utilized this type of trust if you have ever been in a deeply committed relationship, because we don't fall in love with someone we don't believe in. One of the first questions we ask ourselves while dating is, *Can I trust this person with my heart?*

The bottom-line impact of trust was the focus of a 2011 study of 191 teams in Asia and the United States published in the *Journal of Applied Psychology.* Researchers Schaubroeck, Peng, and Chunyan showed an intriguing relationship between trust in leadership and group performance. When trust went up, so did results. But when that trust was what we would classify as character-based, team financial results were better yet—on average 10 percent higher than peer groups.

Building a foundation of capability-based trust begins with establishing the right combination of skills and background. That's not a lengthy process. But once those basic credentials are in place the process of building character-based trust hinges on what you do and say.

Below we offer a few best practices. You'll see it comes down to two salient points: employees must know that you are genuine and know that you care about and respect them.

Show You Are Genuine

Do what's right, regardless of personal risk. Most managers intuitively know what's right in most situations, and yet the allure of money, power, popularity, or promotion often gets in the way of the right decision. Following our first instinct to do the right thing, even ignoring any personal consequences, will nearly always create respect from those around us. And from respect comes trust.

Admit when you're wrong. Leaders who perpetuate the myth that they are infallible create a culture where people around them are afraid to take risks. Hypocrisy such as this breeds resentment and is an innovation killer. Modeling appropriate accountability and demonstrating that mistakes are a cost of doing business (not to mention part of being human) creates a healthy workplace where people feel safe enough to take intelligent chances.

Define the big picture. Helping employees understand the big picture and their role in it provides an artery for information and truth. By communicating the organization's mission, a manager articulates where her team should be heading and emphasizes her personal commitment to that goal. And by constantly communicating values, the methods for getting there are established.

Show You Care About and Respect Your People

Value feedback. Leaders who inspire trust encourage criticism and debate even if it rattles harmony, realizing that only through an honest dialogue with team members, peers, and leaders will the best ideas emerge.

Tell it like it is. Great managers leave the "pillows" at home, the tendency most of us have to soften the blow (and thereby dilute clarity). They have hard conversations with employees and even clients, thus building honest long-term relationships. A singular characteristic of these great leaders is their ability to keep their emotions in check during these discussions while focusing team members on positive outcomes.

Be accessible. Trust is established when even a newcomer, a part-timer, or an entry-level employee quickly feels like a valued member of the team. This begins with managers being available, walking the floor, and avoiding signs of aloofness. It is enhanced when leaders share what they know as soon as they know it, when they seek opinions and ideas, and even through small actions such as getting to know the preferred names of employees and saying a respectful hello every morning.

Don't hog the glory. Giving acknowledgment publicly for great ideas creates perpetual energy among employees, and it encourages such future contributions. And yet one of the most common complaints of untrusting workers is "My boss takes credit for my work."

Focus on shared results. Closely related to the above is putting an emphasis on acknowledging collaborative achievements. Teamwork and trust have a statistically significant correlation. Organizations that score highest in trust also score high in collaboration, according to an Interaction Associates survey of business leaders from 150 companies in industries including health care, energy, financial services, technology, and manufacturing. As Lao-tzu once put it, "A leader is best when . . . his work is done, his aim is fulfilled and the [people] say, 'We did it ourselves.'"

Starbucks helps facilitate an environment of caring and genuineness by giving all of its people equity shares—they call it Bean Stock. When CEO Howard Schultz told this plan to normally stoic Japanese partners (his term for "employees"), many openly wept.

How does Google demonstrate it cares to a group of highly-sought-after programmers and engineers? The firm, often in the top two or three best places to work, gives its technologists 20 percent of their time to work on whatever pet projects intrigue them.

While those ideas may be controlled by corporate policy, we have met a score of high-performing managers who show they care through simpler means: facilitating work-life balance (i.e., "Go home, Ingrid"), helping people prioritize their assignments, making sure their people get all the information they need to do their job and feel secure, and so on.

With a few simple steps, sharing can accelerate trust, and trust can transform your culture.

Step Summary

SHARE EVERYTHING

GENERATING TRUST THROUGH TRANSPARENT COMMUNICATION

- Few things derail a manager's attempts to improve a culture faster than a lack of trust.
- Much of the distrust we see in work groups is a result of misunderstanding or misreading the intentions of others—especially the leader. When information is withheld or not communicated properly, employees tend to suspect the worst and rumors take the place of facts.
- People inevitably build a backstory for leadership decisions, and whether they trust you or not is the most significant determiner of whether that story will be positive or negative.
- While leaders often shy away from discussing hard truths, fearing they will dishearten workers, there's something exhilarating about facing facts head-on, which helps people feel as if they are being brought into the inner circle.
- Through example, leaders can create a contagion of openness that leads first to trust and then to tangible changes in the levels of engagement, enablement, and energy.
- Character-based trust moves an organization forward. It is created by a leader's consistent behavior, adherence to principles, openness, honesty, and dependability.
- Trusted managers can create a psychological belief that the team is a safe place for risk taking, a culture where we can give our all because someone in charge is looking out for us. But employees must know their manager is genuine and cares about and respects them.

8

Partner with Your Talent

What's in It for Me?

A distinguishing quality of great companies is the ability of management at all levels to help employees feel like valued, contributing partners in the business. When you look at this idea from an employee's point of view, the attraction is understandable. But the benefits for businesses are very real too. After all, the worldwide workforce has hidden reserves of ingenuity and resolve that can be tapped. The more your culture spreads the responsibility for corporate success to everyone, the more people feel as if they are an important part of something bigger than themselves, and the more they believe there is a commensurate return for their hard work. And that leads to a culture of high performance.

This idea is about more than including your people in problem solving, which we've already discussed. No, this is bigger. It's about treating your talent as equals in an effort to enhance your culture and help people feel motivated to excel and give you their full effort in every aspect of their work.

The bottom line is this: Your people have more energy and creativity to give. There are employees now in your organization walking around with brilliant ideas in their pocket. Some will never share them because they don't have the platform to launch those ideas on their own. Most, however, will never reveal them because they don't feel like a partner in the organization.

How do you get your people to "empty their pockets"? And here are some bigger and perhaps more probing questions: Why does it feel like so many managers don't want their people to share their ideas? Why don't more managers want their people to feel like partners?

It was refreshing for us to find in Buffalo, New York, an organization that is moving from being very good to what they call "something really special" by getting their people to "empty their pockets."

If you aren't familiar with First Niagara Financial Group (FNFG), you will be soon. They are growing, and fast, with $31 billion in assets and 346 branches with more than 5,000 employees in the northeast United States.

Running a publicly traded, regulated entity, their chief executive officer, John Koelmel, is a busy guy. In 2011, when we began working with FNFG, Koelmel was scheduled to meet with a group of high-potential employees during a leadership-development initiative in Beaver Hollow, New York. Given the CEO's demanding schedule, the group was to get him for twenty minutes.

But when Koelmel arrived he took off his coat, shook every person's hand, rolled up his sleeves, and said, "You are our high-potential people. You are our future. I need to be listening to you." For over an hour, the CEO then proceeded to ask for their honest input about issues, challenges, and opportunities facing them in their roles around the organization. He didn't just listen, he probed, asking great follow-up questions and pushing the group to be more candid. And he took notes on flip charts and then ripped them off one by one and stuck them on the conference room walls. Finally, when the discussion was exhausted, Koelmel took down the giant sheets of paper and rolled them up like an architect's blueprint. He assured the employee group that he had listened, and that he would discuss these ideas the very next day in his management committee meeting and they would get to work. He also promised them that he would report to the group on the progress that was being made.

What impact did this have on these high-potential employees—the very people that a growing bank like First Niagara needs to keep, and keep engaged? Senior Vice President Siobhan Smith was overseeing the meeting. She told us, "They were blown away with his candor [and] ability to listen and capture their thoughts. There wasn't a person in that room that wouldn't have taken a bullet for John when he walked out with those ideas rolled up under his arm."

And, as promised, the next day Koelmel stuck the pages on the wall in front of First Niagara's senior leadership team and they embarked on a discussion of the ideas—ironically most centered around improving the way the bank communicates and how they could better help people feel connected with the organization. The leaders then made assignments and went to work.

It's a story that powerfully represents two core components of why partnering with your talent leads to great effects: It helps your people develop a sense of *connection* and feel a sense of *growth*.

≈ ALL IN ≈

CONNECTION AND GROWTH

Imagine you are a violinist and you have just auditioned for a symphony orchestra. You've dreamed about it since you started taking lessons at age four. You auditioned behind a white sheet to keep your identity from management; you survived numerous sessions with fewer and fewer players competing against you. Finally you got the job (nicely done, by the way). You sit in the last chair playing second violin, but hey, you're in.

If the symphony director, the concertmaster, and your section leader are doing their jobs, pretty soon you start to feel *connected*. This is important because if you don't feel like one of the orchestra, if you don't breathe and play and think like they do, the audience will hear it. This disunity will become audible in performance. Feeling connected means that you understand your role in a piece of music and how it fits into the whole, you think your part is important, and you feel like you are getting two-way feedback on your and your team's performance. You will go from being an anonymous auditioner to someone whom your section leader, concertmaster, and conductor know very well and count on. They will engage you in lively discussions about the music, value your opinion, and give you feedback during rehearsals and after performances.

Again, if your leaders are doing their jobs, soon you'll also feel a sense of *growth*. Even though it can be a great challenge to not get lax as you play Beethoven's Fifth for what seems like the eight hundredth time, you mature as a musician because new conductors bring fresh interpretations to the music and you find yourself seeing new ideas in scores that you thought you knew inside and out. Also, although you start out at the back of the orchestra, as you build experience and ability, you see that you could evolve perhaps into a first chair one day. You also see that most of the talented musicians around you stay, and you feel like you are getting honest feedback, advanced training, and encouragement to experiment and get better.

The orchestra gets better too, and this makes you work even harder. When everything is going well—when reviews are positive, when concerts are sold out, when the orchestra attracts the best players, when all of the members of the symphony feel as if they have momentum—then truly superior performances are achieved.

No matter if you run an orchestra or a business team, a department or a division, employee feelings of connection and growth result from your partnering with them. And yet creating a work environment like we've described, where workers are actively encouraged to reach their highest potential, can rub some managers the wrong way. Why? Because to get people to care, managers must create a WIIFM, or "what's in it for me," for each person.

We would be hard pressed to name a successful executive we've encountered in our travels who hadn't put considerable thought into delivering value to his or her customers. The trouble is, very few leaders spend much time answering what's-in-it-for-me questions for their employees—the people who serve those customers with either energy and smiles or grudging reluctance. *We still pay them, don't we? The checks are still going out, right?* These are real questions we've heard when we raise this subject, attitudes that kill any sense of connection or growth. People can get a paycheck anywhere. They stay, and stay connected, in cultures where they feel they can make a difference.

We recently learned about an unusual organization that has learned this lesson of partnering and has experienced great results. We spoke with Rich Gorman, the chief operating officer of the U.S. Army's Family and MWR Command. His organization has 30,000 employees who provide soldiers and their families with social, fitness, recreational, and other activities, including armed forces resort hotels located around the world.

Gorman told us that just four years ago, the command's annual employee turnover was 47 percent and their customer satisfaction scores weren't anything to write home about. "We knew we had to do better in customer service, but it was difficult when we were rehiring half our workforce every year. Our customer service course helped, but only for so long. For the three weeks after, our client comments improved but then declined again. The problem was, the culture hadn't changed."

Leaders discovered that creating a more effective customer service culture had less to do with focusing on how they took care of their customers and more with how they took care of their employees. Gorman added, "As managers we are here to elicit excellence in service, but we can't order it. We can order them to be satisfactory, and we can correct or even fire them if they aren't. But we can't make them be excellent. That is their choice."

Thus, the command began a program of putting employees in a position for success by ensuring each person has clear expectations, reasonable training, proper equipment, and celebrations for successes—they call that last idea "caught doing something good."

There's a similar philosophy at work at the Container Store, where CEO Kip Tindell says, "If you take better care of the employee than everyone else, [they] take better care of the customer and wonderfully and ironically the shareholder will be happy too."

At the Container Store, despite competing in a cutthroat retail environment well known for low wages and tough working conditions, average pay for a floor salesperson is $46,000, and the company offers health benefits to even part-time employees. The chain also invests heavily in its people, providing an average of 260 hours of training, a whopping thirty times the industry average.

"When you are selling empty boxes, you'd better have great people," said Tindell. "You walk in the store and you can feel it. Everyone loves to be here. Employees. Customers."

And when the Great Recession hit retail hard, Tindell leveled with employees, who agreed to freeze their salaries and 401(k) match for a while in order to save coworkers' jobs. He calls their way of partnering with their talent "conscientious capitalism" and says, "We're not just being nice; it's a successful profit strategy."

≈ ALL IN ≈

CLARIFY CAREER OPPORTUNITIES

Likewise, in the American Express facility in Fort Lauderdale we found a large organization that is recognized as the best in the world at what it does through clear devotion to solving customer needs but an equally fierce commitment to creating a rich environment for their people. And in an ironic twist, the more these employees receive, the more they give to those they serve.

A foundational idea in developing a partnership with your people is taking an active and ongoing role in clarifying growth avenues and career opportunities. Says Vice President Dean Vocaturo, "Some of my people may want to move up and become the next vice president of billing and payment. Some just want to have solid employment here. But some may aspire to be a nurse, a teacher, or a carpenter. Whatever they want to do, I tell my team leaders, 'It's your job to understand what their ambitions are and help support them to get there. It will pay back tenfold.'"

Adds AmEx director Catherine Cole, "I think every day about my greater purpose, what I'm here for. I'm not in social services, I'm not a doctor or nurse, I'm not saving lives. But I take what I do very seriously. I believe my greater purpose is making my people feel good about what they do and to help them work on things they don't have confidence in at this time—to accelerate their careers. My job is to develop better leaders and better people."

Great managers ensure that individuals have opportunities and challenges to rise to their personal best. After all, we all want something to strive for—we need that WIIFM, or personal benefit, to our work. It doesn't take long to talk with each team member to find out who hopes to rise to the next level and who is more interested in staying put but expanding their skill set.

This brings to mind a recent conversation we had with Mark Lindstrom, vice president of operations for the Coffee Bean and Tea Leaf, one of the world's largest privately owned coffee and tea businesses, with eight hundred stores in twenty-two countries. Despite being almost fifty years old, the company has seen same-store sales increase an average of 15 percent in the last two years, and much of that whopping success has come by creating a true team mentality with managers and their people.

When Lindstrom joined the firm two years ago, he knew the seeds of greatness were there. For instance, he met with Nicole Scott, the general manager of one of the stores in Los Angeles. When he asked her to explain her job, Scott's answer floored him. She didn't talk about product quality or customer satisfaction, at least not at first, but said, "My role is to get my team members to fall in love with our company and their jobs, just like I have."

To that end, leaders throughout that organization are now on a mission to develop more talented GMs and district managers internally, rather than having to look outside for new leaders as they grow.

A question to ask yourself is this: Do your team members even understand the levels above them and what is realistically needed to get there?

In one of his first meetings with new employees, Scott O'Neil, president of Madison Square Garden Sports in New York City, told us that he asks, "Where do you want to be five years from now?" He then explains he'll make a commitment to help the person achieve their dream . . . but only if they commit to giving their very best every day. Who wouldn't make that promise after such a one-on-one from a powerful leader like O'Neil? And what's more, they know he delivers. Today, there are executives all over the sports world who got help from Scott O'Neil.

What we find is that people who are engaged, enabled, and energized rarely want to stay stagnant. That might not necessarily mean promotions and climbing the corporate ladder. Instead, effective managers communicate areas of potential growth and learning, so employees can achieve personal goals and continue to reach for higher levels of competency and impact.

A core result of all of this is retention—especially of your most talented people. In cultures where employees are treated like true partners, the best people stay—and stay committed. We've found in our surveys that a red flag for a culture is when talented employees start leaving. Involuntary attrition of star performers is something you can't hide from anyone—fellow employees or even customers.

If you can follow these simple steps to creating a true sense of partnership with employees, turnover can be managed. After all, people generally do want to stay, especially in this economy. While not considered a highly rated motivator of employee attitudes even a few years ago, new data finds the desire for job security trumps most other factors right now. Some 76 percent of employees want a secure and stable position "above all else." Currently only a third of employees globally define themselves as "job hoppers," and that percentage drops dramatically in many countries—counterintuitively in parts of Europe and North America where you might think workers would have more options than in developing countries. In addition, confidence in job security is fairly low, again most particularly in the most mature economies hardest hit by the recession.

A critical first step in building a strong partnership is for managers to take a fresh look at the concept of security. This may involve drawing a line between old-style "passive" security—the "take care of me" mantra of days past—and the "equip me to do it myself" type of security today's knowledge workers are seeking. Equipping employees with the capabilities and tools to secure their own futures will clearly make them feel enabled, but it will also make them feel more engaged and energized.

Here is a listing of key ways in which managers can generate more of a partnership feeling in their culture:

Daily involvement. In the best workplaces, brainstorming and team collaboration are everyday exercises. These actions not only make employees feel involved and appreciated for their ingenuity, but they also initiate a perpetual focus on improvement for the future instead of constantly responding to the present. Make sure a portion of every staff meeting is spent engaging your team in a discussion about new ideas, threats, opportunities, and where you are going together.

Seek personal improvement. In the best cultures, managers provide a glimpse of where each individual team member could be headed. And linked to that idea, they ensure employees not only take on but complete challenging tasks and projects within deadline, spurring growth. Personal improvement also occurs through education, taking on a new project, awareness of areas to improve, or even greater social interaction. As one manager said, his career only took off after his leader encouraged him to have lunch once a week with other managers from around the company.

Just listen. For a leader, it's always nice to hear positive feedback from our employees. "Boss, things are going well, your ideas are being implemented, and your strategy seems right on track." Unfortunately, none of us lives in a Disney movie. Often our concepts could use some improvement, our direction might be flawed, or perhaps we've taken our eyes off our customers' needs. To create a true partnership, we need our employees to know we are listening—and we need to know when something isn't working. Too many leaders aren't willing to really listen to negative feedback from their people. We call them Management Fascists. They think they're open, but in reality they suppress all contrary or opposing views. The ability to allow disagreement, without taking offense, is essential. When dissent is discouraged, people disengage.

Give in. So many managers do it: When it comes to critiquing employee work, they impose their personal preferences, e.g., "Johnson, any professional knows a *good* report features the use of pie charts." Allowing employees to insert their style and creativity into an assignment without unnecessary censorship demonstrates trust in employees' abilities. And the experience of taking the lead builds competency, a sense of ownership, and trust in you as a leader. Look, we know it's hard to hold back criticism, and a manager wants to always be right, but a good rule of thumb is, "If it's 70 percent as good as you would have done it, then leave it alone."

Step Summary

PARTNER WITH YOUR TALENT
WHAT'S IN IT FOR ME?

- A distinguishing quality of great companies is the ability of management at all levels to help employees feel like valued, contributing partners in the business. These cultures spread the responsibility for corporate success to everyone, and also the rewards.
- Your people have more energy and creativity to give. Your employees have brilliant ideas in their pocket that they will never reveal if they don't feel like a partner in the organization.
- Effective managers help create feelings of *connection* and *growth* in their employees. They create a WIIFM, or "what's in it for me," for each person.
- A foundational idea is taking an active and ongoing role in clarifying growth avenues and career opportunities. After all, people who are engaged, enabled, and energized rarely want to be stagnant.
- People want to stay with you. While not considered a highly rated motivator of employee attitudes even a few years ago, new data finds the desire for job security trumps most other factors right now.
- In cultures where employees are treated like true partners, the best people stay—and stay committed.
- A question to ask yourself: Do your team members understand the levels above them and what is realistically needed to get there?

9

Root for Each Other

Develop a Culture of Appreciation and Goodwill

A few years ago we received a call from the newly appointed leader of a very large, very productive IT group. He wanted us to give a talk in front of his entire division—"I need all my people to understand the basics of thanking each other," he said. We told him we'd be delighted and added that we were thrilled that he was inviting all his employees to the gathering, not just his managers, as everyone should learn how to root for each other.

"Oh, they know *how*," he said. "That's the problem. I need them to understand that they are thanking each other too much. We are spending a fortune on recognition."

There was silence on our end of the line as we thought this through. While we hate to say no to an opportunity to teach a group, what he was suggesting from us was akin to asking Casanova to give a lecture on abstinence. In our travels we rarely meet a work group that is saying thanks anywhere near enough, let alone one that is giving too much appreciation. This leader had just inherited an industrious, cheerful place, and he saw spending on peer-to-peer and top-down recognition as one line item he could tighten up on to further enhance efficiency.

Was he ever barking up the wrong tree.

Most managers want to create cultures where their teams perform up to capacity, but few grasp that for a culture to really take off, teammates must encourage each other on a daily basis. More so, colleagues must be *empowered* to support one another even when situations aren't ideal—such as when a boss is too busy, when there is outright dysfunction above, or when there are overwhelming deadlines—so that the entire organization doesn't topple like dominoes.

The answer is in rooting for each other: having each other's backs, appreciating strengths, and recognizing what we value the most about each other—for every worker on every line, in the field, behind every desk, answering every phone call. Cultures are communal, after all.

It would be a mistake to confuse this kind of qualitative appreciation, which happens on a daily, moment-to-moment basis, with providing incentives. It's certainly true that business managers can get their people to do almost anything with the right incentive. People will practically kill themselves for a once-in-a-lifetime opportunity—a large cash bonus, for instance. But that's not sustainable. What happens the day after the cash is paid? Employees can't maintain the overdrive pace. They can burn out, can disengage, and may even become disruptive or quit. The alternative is a stronger focus on the people themselves and their individual motivations and strengths. As Thomas Carlyle said, "The great law of culture is: Let each become all that he was capable of being . . . and show himself at length in his own shape and stature, be these what they may."

Our research shows incontrovertible evidence that employees respond best when they are recognized for things they are good at *and* for those actions where they had to stretch. It is this reinforcement that makes people want to grow to their full shape and stature, as Carlyle put it. And to know they are on the right path, workers need acknowledgment not only from their immediate bosses, but also from their peers.

≈ ALL IN ≈

THE DEMOCRATIZATION OF RECOGNITION

Many companies in recent years have amped up the top-down type of praise, and we applaud their efforts, but manager-to-employee and peer-to-peer recognition fulfill separate human needs. Workers want to know that their bosses see their effort and truly value it. This ties in to feelings of job security and well-being and opportunities for development. But employees also need the affirmation that their coworkers see them as trustworthy, dependable, and creative. This reinforces that you have friends at work, that you are accepted, and that others have your back. Repeatedly in surveys, the most engaged employees say things such as "My manager recognizes my above-and-beyond work" or "I feel praised for my contributions," but also, "My teammates support each other."

When we visited Zappos.com headquarters in Las Vegas, leaders outlined for us a healthy number of recognition programs in use, and yet all but one or two were peer-to-peer. For instance, call center managers Rob Siefker and Maura Sullivan told us about SNAPS recognition, which happens in their customer loyalty teams. "SNAPS" stands for "Super Nifty And Positive Stuff."

Siefker said, "The lead supervisors and managers hold Zuddles [Zappos huddles] with our teams at nine fifteen and three fifteen on Tuesdays and Thursdays. It's quick—what's going on in the call center, are there any big-ticket items we need to discuss, big news that we need to pass down—and then at the end we do SNAPS. There's a little box in the call center and people write things that someone else did that was really cool. These are read during the Zuddles and then the person is publicly recognized on the spot. It's peer-to-peer. Then we all snap our fingers." (Sullivan and Siefker both demonstrated for us and we couldn't help laughing with them—it's 1950s Greenwich Village poetry-reading cool.)

Added Sullivan, "It's been a fun way to make sure we're recognizing each other, even for the little things, the things that make a difference culturally for our environment." Of course, like every business Zappos faces challenges: Competitors are relentless, Wall Street is demanding, and customers must be served. But the leadership has seen the value of making time for employees to have fun rooting for each other this way.

What we are describing here is an entire ecosystem of appreciation and rooting for each other that mitigates natural infighting and jealousies. Imagine going to work in a landscape like this. The work is demanding, of course, but it's paced in a way that is sustainable. Along the way, you are encouraged by not only your boss but your coworkers. If you make a mistake, you get immediate feedback for improvement and perhaps a sincere pat on the back for taking a risk. There are celebrated milestones everywhere that keep you glued to your job. You want to stay and make a difference with people you like and who like you.

This idea of workers rooting for each other usually requires a transformational change of mind-set in organizations. But we have found these affirming atmospheres firsthand on every continent we've visited and it's a wondrous thing to witness. It's fun to work in these places and people are happier, yet there's much more. The spirit of competition is alive and kicking, but instead of battling against each other for attention from management, employees work together and encourage each other as they make their business more competitive against outside forces.

You might be skeptical that real workplaces such as this even exist, where employees regularly stop their work to gather teammates together to thank them publicly, where immediate supervisors are empowered to appreciate employees with tangible awards. So let's return for the last time to the call center in Fort Lauderdale to study again Doria Camaraza's three-thousand-person team at American Express.

While these employees in Florida are not working in particularly glamorous jobs, we were amazed at the hip and happening rooting culture that the organization has developed and how its actions play out in real time. A large part of the executive group's commitment to developing their people includes recognizing individual contributions when people stretch and grow. In fact, there is more individual, team, top-down, and peer-to-peer appreciation here than we've ever seen in a workplace.

All of this recognition is part of a multipronged, multiyear approach to enhancing performance and loyalty throughout American Express's 59,000-person global enterprise. Over the last few years we've watched a team of leaders—David Kasiarz, Jim Dwyer, Rebecca Winslow Booth, and Lauren Torio—diligently create the tools managers need to reward their people around the world, and it's been exciting to see these tools, and many others, in action.

Below are a few highlights from the list that leaders gave us. It filled up four flip charts and a whiteboard. They call the entire process "holding up your heroes." Their efforts are divided between daily, monthly, and annual opportunities for recognition.

Daily Recognition

- RewardBlue—American Express maintains a global recognition system where any employee can recognize any other employee in forty-five countries using:
  - ❏ E-cards and E-buttons (online thank-yous that recognize leadership, birthdays, holidays, and great work tied to the AmEx Blue Box Values; thousands of cards will be sent each year by Fort Lauderdale employees alone)
  - ❏ Blue Awards (paid into an account for above-and-beyond work; can be accumulated and later redeemed for merchandise, AmEx gift cards, or cash)
- RewardBlue Loyalty—American Express acknowledges years of service with a tiered reward system:
  - ❏ Every five years of service employees are recognized with an award and the image of an AmEx credit card etched in crystal.
  - ❏ Leaders recognize anniversaries through team meetings or

town halls (these presentations are happening almost daily in Fort Lauderdale).

◻ Employees with more than twenty-five years of service join the Quarter Century Club, with benefits (including yearly banquet dinners) lasting until retirement. Employees with more than thirty-five years of service receive an experiential award, such as tickets to a sought-after sporting event or a weekend at a resort in a fun location.

- Power Hour—The company dedicates time during the day to recognize and energize a specific team.
- Shift Turnover—The organization recognizes the best performer at the end of the shift.
- Spin the Wheel—AmEx allows those who are caught living the values to spin a wheel on the floor for prizes such as movie tickets or lunch passes.
- Face-to-face Praise—Company leaders spend 75 percent of their time on the floor. A key reason is to identify and appreciate great behaviors on the spot.
- Complimentary Letters from Customers—The teams are gathered and letters are read aloud. The named team members are recognized.
- Birthdays and Special Events—Despite extreme production schedules, celebrations spring up regularly in each team.

Monthly Recognition

- Tribute—In the Fort Lauderdale offices, the organization holds a dance party in Camaraza's atrium for the entire center to pay tribute to above-and-beyond achievements and long tenure.
- Business Town Halls—Updates for all employees are held for all three shifts, with recognition awards including parking passes and RewardBlue points for those who live the values.
- Segment Winners—Teams from all global locations compete to be ranked at the top of their business segment each month.

The winning employees are treated to lunch and are recognized by leaders.

- Most Valuable Player—The top-ranked employees and top team leaders in each segment are recognized during a department celebration and are given a pass for a free lunch or free movie tickets.
- White Glove Lunches—Top performers in Fort Lauderdale's dispute department are treated to a formal lunch served by their leaders.
- Dish with Doria—The general manager has lunch with randomly selected employees from each of the major divisions to hear honest feedback.

Annual Recognition

- Chairman's Award for Innovation—A company-wide award recognizing employee teams that demonstrate innovation in growing the business or redefining American Express. There are two levels:
  - ❏ Chairman's Award Finalists—About twenty-five teams are selected by their business/staff units as Chairman's Award finalists. Team members each receive $1,000.
  - ❏ Chairman's Award Winners—As many as six teams are selected from among the finalists. Each member of the winning teams receives an additional $3,000.
- World Service Excellence Award—This award recognizes employees for exceptional achievements and those who exemplify the attributes that drive the organization's ongoing success. Criteria center on the company's mantra of "Deliver Superior Service, Drive Efficiency, Drive Growth," and an additional important attribute, "superior leadership." Honorees receive RewardBlue awards and are celebrated during senior-leader-hosted regional luncheons.
- Superior Performance Award—This award recognizes contributions to the business as measured through the annual

performance-management process. All employees—from customer care professionals to directors—who receive the highest annual performance evaluation ratings are eligible to attend the celebration.

- American Express Customer Service Award—This recognition targets frontline customer care and customer-facing professionals who go to exceptional lengths to provide outstanding service to customers. One of two awards sponsored by CEO Ken Chenault, it recognizes employees who provided an act of outstanding service over the past year and those employees who demonstrate consistent excellence over five years or more. Winners each receive $4,000, a crystal award, and an all-expense-paid trip to New York City with a guest. Winners are also recognized locally.

It's a prodigious list, isn't it? And this is just a partial cataloging of what they are doing. When we finished taking notes on the sheets and the leaders could see the scope of what they do for employees, General Manager Camaraza chuckled and said, "I really had no idea we were doing this much. It's pretty amazing when you see it all."

And yet there was more. Catherine Cole, a director, said, "On our team we have a 'fuddle,' a fun huddle where we take people away from the work once a month for about twenty minutes and do something like play a game to help them decompress. We want everyone to know how valuable their work is and we want them to feel good about showing up here every day."

Doug DiPaola looked at the list and added an idea relating to AmEx's annual winning of five consecutive J. D. Power & Associates awards for customer satisfaction. "J. D. Power is something that is great recognition externally, but if you don't have a culture of celebrating successes along the way, then the types of behaviors J. D. Power looks for just don't get reinforced."

Think about what this vice president said for just a moment. It seems so elementary, doesn't it? Then why do so many leaders have a hard time grasping the concept that publicly recognizing the right behaviors leads us to achieving our corporate objectives?

It might be easy to dismiss all of the above initiatives and say they wouldn't fly in your culture. You could say, "We've tried that and it didn't work," or the more frequent refrain, "We know we should do more, but we are just too busy." What we're saying is that if you want to transform your corporate culture, you don't have to choose these exact programs, but you must do something—despite the challenges.

Even at this American Express facility some have struggled to make this culture of recognition happen given a team's unique circumstances or pressures. For example, we spoke with Todd Schemm, who leads world telephone services. He had a dilemma. He told us, "I believe strongly in energizing the team by recognizing the little things, the successes we see every day. The trouble is my people are on the phone seventy percent of the time, so I don't have a lot of opportunity to pull them off to 'rah-rah.' With inbound telephone service you've constantly got twenty calls in queue, one after another, so how do I provide that opportunity to energize?"

So he asked his team leaders and they said to go mobile. "Each leader has a laptop, and they can listen and roam the floor and immediately connect with their team. They can either send an e-button or say in person, 'That was a great call, and here's why.'"

As for Camaraza, she ends every week with recognition. On Fridays at nine she will log in to the phone system and listen to a number of random calls from the day before. If the call was great, she'll walk up to the floor and recognize the representative on the spot. Or if constructive feedback is needed, she'll give that right away—in person. "I know it creates a little buzz on the floor—'Hey, did you see Doria was here?' That's okay; it shows everyone that I'm listening and really want to catch them doing something great."

≈ ALL IN ≈

TAKE A STEP

Members and leaders of high-functioning teams positively reward even the smallest steps toward desired change, training the brain away from negative associations and replacing them with positive. Several of our previous studies have shown the remarkable impact recognition can have on a business. In *The Carrot Principle,* we showed that organizations most effective at "recognizing excellence" were up to three times more profitable than their peers on return on equity and operating margin. But other measures are impacted as well. For example, after implementing an effective top-down and peer-to-peer recognition program, KPMG LLP, the U.S. audit, tax, and advisory firm, saw positive employee engagement scores on its internal survey increase by 20 twenty points. Not only that, but a survey from Towers Watson found recognition from an immediate supervisor has a dramatic effect in improving low-engagement workplaces. In these environments, strong manager performance in recognizing employee achievement increased engagement by almost 60 percent.

All of our minds are shaped by the power of appreciation. Over time, leaders who frequently create a culture of rooting for their people with positive recognition can undo the hardwiring that causes our minds to be skeptical of those in authority, to fight change, and to look for reasons to feel undervalued. Acts of recognition are investments in the future of your people. As we root, encourage, and celebrate together, we create a resource of goodwill that will yield the benefits of loyalty, dedication, and innovation.

If the process of recognition is intimidating, use the following formula. It's not complicated, and it works for leaders recognizing employees or peers thanking each other.

- **Do it now.** Recognition doesn't age well. The closer recognition follows a desired behavior, the more strongly that action is reinforced.

- **Do it often.** Recognition should be habitual to build a positive culture. In the best workplaces, people feel praised every seven days, according to research from the Gallup Organization.
- **Be specific.** Teammates must clearly understand what behavior triggered the recognition in order to repeat it. For maximum impact, clearly link each recognition event to one of your core values that you wish to see repeated.
- **Be sincere.** Reward only those behaviors you truly value, with a heartfelt and public thank-you. This is all too rare and can be extraordinarily meaningful.

We have spent the past twenty years trying to convince businesspeople that recognition engages teams. Some have listened and prospered; others haven't. The good news is we've seen appreciation done right in some of the world's best companies. This has solidified a culture of constant reinforcement. After all, culture is about behaviors, plain and simple, and recognition is about reinforcing the right behaviors. That's why it is so important to your organization's success.

But on the negative side of the ledger, consider a 2011 survey of working Americans that found 65 percent of people who are otherwise satisfied—those who aren't interested in finding a new job—admit they would work harder if they just received more praise for their efforts.

Case in point: We were on a flight from Las Vegas when we fortuitously overheard a fascinating conversation. The flight attendant who had welcomed us on board was energetic and upbeat, a true ambassador for the airline. He was so atypical, in fact, that the two men seated behind us asked if they could speak to corporate and get him recognized. His good nature faded as he grumbled, "That's nice of you, but please don't bother. We have a recognition system, but you need about three billion points before you can get anything worthwhile. I have maybe two hundred and eighty thousand points, which I think is like a fifty-dollar gift certificate."

Here was an amazing employee who was persevering despite the airline's poor system to thank him. Did he have more to give?

Maybe. Was he dissatisfied, disheartened, and even dismayed with the lack of acknowledgment for his great work—and did that make him a potential turnover risk? Without a doubt.

This recent recognition study found that such a lack of sincere recognition is leading to employee turnover. Some 38 percent of working Americans say they are looking to leave their current companies, and the researchers found a startling correlation between the level of recognition a manager gives and the loyalty of his or her workers.

The problem is this: Few leadership teams are grasping the importance of this issue. As we work with executive groups, most fail to admit the true toll on morale that the prolonged recession has wrought. Without exception, they laid off workers and/or asked for superhuman efforts from their remaining staff. But the level of appreciation has not increased; in fact, it's decreased in most places since leaders are so very busy.

It's time to turn the tide. The power of effective recognition can spread throughout a culture faster than a speeding bullet, creating a place where employees are willing to give their all and put down roots because they know their contributions will be celebrated. A key starting point is making regular award presentations to your staff when they go above and beyond—these happen at least daily in the best teams we studied. A tip: When you or one of your employees presents an award, remember our acronym of STEP:

- Tell a **Story** about the person's accomplishments. What did the person have to overcome, what tough customer issue did they face, etc.
- Gather people **Together.** Praise is public, criticism is private. The team in attendance will learn as much or even more than the person being thanked.
- **Emphasize** one of your core values. Ensure your award ceremonies recognize only results that are important to the organization.
- **Personalize** the moment. What award can you present that the person will value? Where can you hold the presentation

that is meaningful? What colleagues could you invite to add color to the achievement?

Do it right, and you'll see the power of gratitude at work as a culture builder. In energized organizations, managers say, "Thanks for reaching beyond," and peers say, "Thanks for supporting me." And they say it much more frequently than in organizations ranked poor or average. It's this guileless language and recognition of employee effort that make people feel empowered to perform. Good attempts and good attitudes by your employees are to be encouraged, but successes should be celebrated.

Motivators such as praise and recognition are as powerful as the almighty dollar, in some cases even more so. After all, why do super-wealthy filmmakers, musicians, and actors seem to present each other with televised awards every week or two? Because recognition offers respect. Learn from their unabashed galas. The awards are presented in front of their peers (not behind closed doors). They are a surprise. They are symbolic. And the recipient is given time to thank all those who helped along the way, even Mom. In that way, the ripples of recognition extend beyond the original recipient.

This kind of rooting for one another is a vital element in creating a larger culture of belief. An ingrained expectation that good work will be recognized creates an expectation of greatness. What more could you ask for?

Step Summary

ROOT FOR EACH OTHER
DEVELOP A CULTURE OF
APPRECIATION AND GOODWILL

- Employees must be empowered to root for one another even when situations aren't ideal. The key is to help your people recognize what they value most about each other.
- Culture is about behaviors, and recognition is about reinforcing the right behaviors. That's why it is so important to your organization's success.
- All of our minds are shaped by the power of appreciation. Over time, leaders who frequently create a culture of rooting for their people with positive recognition can undo the hardwiring that causes our minds to be skeptical of those in authority, to fight change, and to look for reasons to feel undervalued.
- Top-down and peer-to-peer recognition fulfill separate human needs. The first enhances a sense of job security, of well-being, and that there are opportunities for development. The latter emphasizes that you have friends at work, that you are accepted, and that others have your back.
- The following formula can help leaders recognize employees or help peers thank each other: "Do it now, do it often, be specific, be sincere."
- When presenting awards, remember the acronym STEP: Tell a *story* about the person's accomplishments, gather people *together, emphasize* one of your core values, and *personalize* the moment.

10

Establish Clear Accountability

Turning a Negative into a Positive

When we are asked to name one factor that can safeguard an organization against cultural failure, the answer is: establishing clear accountability. To grow a great culture, you need to cultivate a place where people have to do more than show up and fog a mirror; they have to fulfill promises—not only collectively but individually.

A lack of accountability is one of the most corrosive elements of ineffective work cultures. It shows up in many ways: people failing to take responsibility, missed deadlines, errors in judgment, misunderstandings, overpromising, personal failures, petty disagreements, unfair expectations, and a marshmallow mound of "should have"s.

But accountability is widely misunderstood as being all about the punitive. In the minds of so many in business, accountability is inherently negative. To be "held accountable" generally implies that a rebuke or punishment of some kind is coming. How often do employees get the message that the boss wants to see them and feel a tightening in their stomachs—*Yeah, just give me a minute while I go throw up.*

A few years ago, we were talking to an employee in the hospitality industry who made an important point so simply that we will never forget it: "When I make a mistake," she said, "I'm recognized one hundred percent of the time; when I do something great, I'm not recognized ninety-nine percent of the time." This is true in so many of the places we visit. Think about all the lost opportunities to inspire better performances. What would happen to her workplace if that 1 percent *positive* accountability could be turned into 2, 5, 10, or 20 percent?

The tendency for bosses to rebuke employees instead of rewarding them prevails in so many industries, but perhaps none more so than health care. Here, leaders have a penchant for perfectionism since lives are at stake. It was so bad in one ICU that a young nurse said, "I feel like a nuisance around here. Everything I do seems wrong." She told us confidentially that her nursing supervisor would spend entire shifts berating her and her coworkers but temper it at the end of the day with a "Good job, everyone" as she grabbed her purse to leave. Said the young nurse, "We wait until the glass doors slide open and she can't see our reflection anymore, and then we all give her the finger."

Heavy-handed leadership such as this is not true accountability; it's faultfinding. Holding people accountable is about much more than criticizing them. It is about assigning responsibility with realistic goals, evaluating progress and making positive course corrections at milestones, removing obstacles, and then closing the loop by celebrating successes or honestly and openly evaluating misses.

Part of the problem with so many managers who overemphasize the negative is that they fail to grasp that most employees actually want to be held accountable—as long as the boss not only points out where they are falling short but also expresses true appreciation of where they are contributing. In fact, a key correlator to low morale is when employees see slacking peers who are not held accountable receive just about the same raises, bonuses, rewards, and attaboys as everyone else. Very few high achievers want to work in a place where there are no heroes and no slackers, where no one is held accountable.

Imagine living in the western United States in the mid-1800s. Unless a lawman was standing near you as you shot someone, there was little chance you'd ever be brought to justice. Despite

the movie retellings of deputized horsemen tracking down kill-
ers, in reality very few murderers were ever pursued. Some
modern corporations aren't so dissimilar. As one worker in one
long-standing organization told us with distaste, "Unless you are
caught stealing or looking at pornography on your computer,
you have employment for life." We often enter places where
everyone is treated pretty much the same, no matter their personal contribution, and it is demoralizing for those who want
their work to be noticed as exceptional.

Some managers back off on individual accountability because
they are somehow afraid of the confrontational side of the
issue. But the truth is, a lack of accountability actually frus-
trates employees just as much as it does you. A profound truth
that all managers should internalize is that more than anything
else, employees really do want to do a good job, and holding
them accountable is an important way we help them do just
that. When accountability is instituted in positive ways, it helps
people feel the satisfaction of achieving a goal and performing
up to (or even surpassing) expectations. But it also allows them
to clearly understand when they're falling short and where they
need to improve. Accountability helps people grow, and that is a
deeply rewarding experience for employees and managers.

Healthy accountability is established according to this cascad-
ing process:

1. An organization decides upon clear, understandable big-
picture goals. Managers are responsible to deliver a team's share
of that goal, and employees are responsible for a worker's share
of the team goal. All parties must buy in, and everyone must
understand what rewards are available if they succeed and what
consequences await if they don't. The journey then begins.

2. Along the way, the organization ensures managers are measured against their goals, and managers do the same for their
employees. There are frequent, measurable milestones where feedback, coaching, and praise are given top-down and bottom-up.

3. At the end of the evaluation cycle, leaders close the loop by assessing success together with their employees. Failures should not be a surprise to either party but are dealt with honestly and directly. Successes are genuinely celebrated.

The entire process is not unlike good parenting. Anyone who has ever been a loving mom, dad, aunt, uncle, or grandparent knows the importance of being an example if you want your kids to follow your advice. The same is true of managers. They must hold themselves accountable in this flow and also to their own goals, clearly and without any hypocrisy.

Likewise, just as in parenting, a key in implementing accountability is finding a balance between flexibility and compassion on the one hand and tough love on the other. Let's say you have an employee who who repeatedly shows up late, and you run a retail store where reliability is much more important than if you ran, for example, a software company that might allow people to come and go liberally. The late employee isn't holding up her end of the bargain, but you know she is a single mom juggling three kids. What do you do? You would be justified in taking draconian action, but should you?

In a situation like this, it's important to acknowledge that people who are showing up late or breaking another simple rule might not be fundamentally irresponsible. Perhaps in the past, managers failed to hold them accountable for slacking off in this way. They might just need to be given a wake-up call (not necessarily literally, but maybe). Compassion and a consideration of people's prior experiences must enter into the accountability equation. The system has to be built for human beings, however fallible they may be.

We are in no way suggesting you become a pushover or that you fail to point out problems; there's enough of that going around. While Hollywood likes to portray most bosses as malevolent, demanding, and tough as nails, in reality we meet a host of managers who are just the opposite. They're promoted into positions of authority because they're good at what they do, but then they have a really, really hard time holding anyone accountable. They feel so uncomfortable with confrontation that they simply avoid unpleasant conversations with their people and just hope workers will be grown-ups and meet their goals. Hope is not a strategy.

People are motivated best when managers strike a good balance. Here's a terrific little example we stumbled upon in our interviews.

Brett Fischer is director of merchandising of Major League Soccer team Real Salt Lake (which you'll learn more about in the next chapter). Fischer's main job is to run the team store. We visited him in the spring of 2011 the day after the team hosted the Central and North American club championship. More than 20,700 fans had crammed into the stadium to cheer on their team. Fischer had assigned bubbly part-time worker Carol to one of the cash registers and she was engaging with each guest, asking them a question or two, making a connection, leaving them smiling with her contagious energy. Normally, this would be great behavior in a cashier, right? But on this big game day her conversations were slowing the line down. People were lined up seven or eight deep, and some were getting visibly anxious about missing the action. So manager Fischer had to act.

He pulled her aside and said, "Carol, it's great that you want to talk with customers, but we really need to find a sense of urgency on the register. So our options are to do a lineup change to put someone else on the register and allow you to engage more with customers on the floor, or you need to focus on getting that till to go a hundred miles an hour."

"My goal was to be tough on the principle but kind on the person," said Fischer. "Her reaction was tender at first. She thought I was criticizing her. But I kept bringing it back to a business need, to what the customers needed, and she eventually said, 'I want to stay on the register; I can do it.'"

Fischer checked on Carol twice more in the three hours that followed. Her line was humming. Her boss had helped her realize she wasn't doing anything doing wrong by interacting with customers, she just needed to balance it with the need for speed on that particular day. "By the end of the game, Carol had run thirteen thousand dollars on the credit card machine and she left feeling like a million bucks," Fischer said.

It's an admittedly modest interaction, but aren't most in your teams? Fischer set a vision for his employee and provided honest feedback and a course correction. He provided coaching in a way that demonstrated he cared about Carol. He knew she had a tender heart and might react negatively to his correction, and indeed she did. How many managers would either buckle at that point or, worse, tell her to get over it? Fischer didn't shirk his duty, nor did he reprimand sternly. He provided options for her to choose from, he kept the conversation focused on customers and what they needed, and he gave the coaching in a kindly manner.

≈ ALL IN ≈

IN ALL FAIRNESS

Accountability like this is at its most basic level about fairness. You owe something; you pay something. It is a settling of debts. With any luck, the two parties agree in advance and the repayment follows their expectations. All business is built on transactions, especially the agreement between employer and employee. And here is where the importance of managers also holding themselves fairly accountable comes in. If a manager doesn't live up to his side and acknowledge his part in failures that might be happening, employees will develop deep resentment of the hypocrisy at play. Think of the employee who says to herself, *You want me to reach my goal, but you've asked me to do twelve other things. Why don't you hold yourself accountable for throwing me off track?*

Here's a little tale to bring this point home. It appeared in *The American Spelling Book,* written by Noah Webster in the late 1700s, and was studied by nearly every American child for generations.

A FARMER came to a neighboring Lawyer, expressing great concern for an accident, which, he said, had just happened.

"One of your oxen," continued he, "has been gored by a bull of mine, and I should be glad to know how I am to make you reparation."

"Thou art a very honest fellow," replied the Lawyer, "and wilt not think it unreasonable that I expect one of your oxen in return."

"It is no more than justice," quoth the Farmer, "to be sure: but what did I say? I mistake—It is your bull that has killed one of my oxen."

"Indeed!" says the Lawyer, "that alters the case: I will enquire into the affair; and if—"

"And if!" said the Farmer—"the business I find would have been concluded without an 'if' had you been as ready to do justice to others, as to extract it from them."

This fable, so influential in its era, was told to illustrate the importance of personal accountability, especially for those who rise to positions of authority. In a way, it's a cynical story. It highlights the views of the day (which persist even now)—namely, that life isn't always fair to those in subordinate positions and that people in power exercise more rights than others. That is, accountability skews to the rich and powerful, and bosses can change the rules as they see fit. If this is true in an organization, it can be terribly corrosive.

A lot of business leaders talk about fair accountability, but seeing it in action is rare. We witnessed a great case in the summer of 2011 in Greenville, North Carolina, when Brian Floyd made a remarkable promise to his 6,000 employees. During a series of town hall meetings, the new chief operating officer of Pitt County Memorial Hospital told workers that if employee engagement scores weren't higher in a year, he wouldn't deserve to be there anymore. If you're like us, you probably can't remember meeting a senior leader who cared that much or who was willing to accept that much personal accountability for his people or his organization.

Medically, Pitt County is a great place to seek care; it's also a good place to work. But Floyd and his fellow leaders wanted to get better at both metrics. As for the COO's bold statement— that he shouldn't be there if he can't build a stronger culture— understand he isn't a guy nearing retirement who has nothing to lose. He's an up-and-coming executive who believes that a primary role of a senior leader is to improve the workplace for employees. And if he can't, he'll let someone else take a shot. That's a leader embracing accountability.

We have found the following components are essential if a leader wants to establish effective accountability in an organization:

The plan. It might sound obvious to start here, but good, clear team plans are rare. It's amazing how real results start happening only after managers meet with their people and collectively put a road map down on paper. Financial targets, customer satisfaction goals, new products launched, and clients to be served all fall out of a clear plan that everyone buys into.

SMART goals. To meet an obligation, all parties have to know who's responsible for what. Keep in mind the well-tested acronym SMART: specific, measurable, attainable, relevant, and timely. Goals need all five qualities to work.

Rules of the game. Accountability presupposes that there are very clear rules in place that have been agreed upon by all parties. One is agreeing to measure progress formally (with performance evaluations, progress reports, and other statistical assessments) and informally (with frequent face-to-face discussions or even e-mail updates). Stanley Hainsworth, owner of the design agency Tether Inc. in Seattle, told us in addition to formal midyear and year-end performance reviews, he holds monthly one-on-one "previews" that give him and his employees the

chance to evaluate progress toward goals and make course corrections smack-dab in between bigger milestones. These don't
need to take place in a formal work environment either; he often
takes his people out to lunch or hits a bucket of balls with them
while chatting.

Monitor progress two ways. You are the boss, so it's okay to
gather data on the progress of your people's initiatives. This isn't
an invitation to create a police state, merely an acknowledgment
that everybody responds to a checkup now and then. A manager should ensure that everyone is still on the same page—for
instance, have your employees been pulled in new directions?
What new obstacles are they facing? Seeking feedback both
ways adds credibility to management and contributes to a worker's willingness to be judged.

Realize the rules or players may change. Now and then rules
change—and they occasionally will as conditions alter—but
management and workers need to agree to any changes. Buy-in
enters the picture again. And don't forget leaders can get all participants on the same page only to have employees depart and
others arrive to take their place. The new people have to enter
into the agreement too, and they might need additional ramp-
up time.

Hit deadlines. People feel as if they are being treated justly when
they can see on paper that their work is due. It comes as no surprise. And just like we had to cram in school to get things turned
in on time, there will be bubbles of busyness in employees' work
lives that require them to push down on the accelerator. It's your
job to point out when those times are coming up.

Have tough conversations. The biggest problem we hear with
accountability is a manager's unwillingness to have tough conversations with employees who are failing—*But she's so loyal
and she tries so hard.* Great managers realize they aren't doing

their employees any favors by letting them slide through their work lives. As we ask employees about the best managers they've ever worked for, they almost always tell us about bosses who were honest, fair, and trusted, and yet asked a ton from them; we never hear about pushovers being favorites.

Be the change. As Brian Floyd showed his employees at Pitt County Memorial Hospital, in building this expectation of accountability a manager has to prove that he is accountable, too. The great leaders we meet aren't afraid to list their goals publicly on a weekly, quarterly, and annual basis. In this way a leader's own values are corroborated by his actions.

Reap the rewards. If as a manager you are spending more time on the dark side of things—finding mistakes, criticizing, and trying to light a fire by force—turn the culture around by devoting much more time to finding what your people are doing right. We made this point in the last chapter, but it bears repeating since it is so often underestimated. No matter how big your organization, a small business with five employees or one with half a million, people expect to be rewarded for their labors when they hold up their end of the bargain. Yes, you can send out a teamwide "Thank you, everyone!" but that motivates exactly no one. True satisfaction comes from one-on-one appreciation for a job well done. It closes the loop. After almost twenty years now, our work has disproved the great myth that giving someone a paycheck fulfills the leadership obligation. Sincere recognition is the final key to establishing a culture of positive accountability.

Let us share with you one last great example of an ethic of accountability having permeated a culture, which we heard about at the corporate offices of one of the world's largest service organizations. At the firm, when someone "walked the talk"—in other words, held themselves accountable and fulfilled a promise—the chairman presented a Walk the Talk award, a two-dollar novelty-store set of chattering teeth. That got our attention. It might seem like a silly prize from a chairman, but nothing could have been further from the truth. As we toured the organization's cubicle maze, we noticed sets of the chattering teeth were everywhere, and always in positions of honor. One employee had even attached dramatic lighting to her cube wall to illuminate her three sets of plastic teeth to best effect.

The company also had what they called a "walk-the-talk band," comprised of bongo drummers, a host of kazooists, and even a sousaphone player. When a Walk the Talk award was presented, the band marched throughout the cubicle maze at corporate headquarters. It was their version of a ticker-tape parade. Several employees told us that they had unsuccessfully fought back tears of joy when first paid a visit by the chairman and the band.

The plot thickens (and thus the reason for the corporation's anonymity).

One day, into this jolly, accountable environment came a new chief financial officer. This head accountant first heard the boisterous band one afternoon while on a conference call with Wall Street. He was mortified. *How utterly unprofessional,* he thought. He slammed his door shut and sat in his office for hours afterward, fuming. He didn't notice the chairman leading the parade.

At the next leadership meeting, the chairman asked if anyone had any other business for the quorum. The new CFO cleared his throat and began. "Look," he said, "I don't know if you know this, but there's a kazoo and bongo group that marches around here. I was on the phone with an analyst last week. We're discussing a million-dollar stock purchase and this goofy band marches by. It was embarrassing."

The room fell silent. People squirmed in their seats. Finally the chairman rose. He spoke with strength. "I don't know if you've noticed our list of values posted on the walls everywhere, but one of the values is we 'walk the talk.' I guess you didn't see that I was at the head of that marching band, presenting a Walk the

Talk award in what we think is a really *fun* way. We can't pay Wall Street salaries here. We may not offer our people company cars or a lot of stock options. But we keep employees because we live our value of accountability and we have fun doing it."

The chairman then added, "And if you don't get that, maybe *you* are in the wrong place."

As it turns out, the new executive *was* in the wrong place. About two months later he decided to leave the organization. He found a place without kazoos and chattering teeth, one that most likely didn't have such a fun way to close the loop on accountability.

Step Summary

ESTABLISH CLEAR ACCOUNTABILITY
TURNING A NEGATIVE INTO A POSITIVE

- A lack of accountability is one of the most corrosive elements of ineffective work cultures and leads to people failing to take responsibility, missed deadlines, errors in judgment, misunderstandings, overpromising, disagreements, and so on.
- Heavy-handed leadership is not accountability but faultfinding. A secret of leadership is in finding a balance.
- When accountability is instituted in positive ways, it helps people feel the satisfaction of achieving a goal and performing up to expectations. It also allows them to understand when they're falling short and where improvements are needed.
- Cultures that treat everyone the same, no matter their personal contribution, are demoralizing for high achievers.
- The following components can help managers establish effective accountability: Start with a clear team plan; assign SMART goals to each person; ensure all parties agree upon the rules, and if something changes, reset and get buy-in again; monitor progress at each step; hit deadlines, and have tough conversations if your people don't; and devote much more time to finding what your people are doing right than finding what they're doing wrong.
- Finally, if a manager doesn't hold himself accountable, and if he doesn't acknowledge his part in failures, employees can develop resentment of the hypocrisy.

Part III

Culture Tools

Dealing with Challenges;
Ideas to Maintain Success

11

Renewing Belief

Rebuilding a Culture in Crisis

Temporary loss of belief of is inevitable in any dynamic, growing organization. The hiring of a new CEO, a merger or acquisition, an evolution from private to public status, or a new competitor in your market all can throw even the most effective culture into a tailspin and shake employee confidence. Or consider what happens in an organization when it suffers from a public scandal, bad press, weakening revenues, a sinking stock price, or uncertainty about leadership's health. Ironically, it is the very moment of crisis when the organization needs its people to believe the most and yet their faith is challenged. Put yourself in the shoes of an oil company employee during a massive spill, a financial services worker whose company is under siege by regulators, a manufacturing employee whose firm faces an embarrassing product recall, or a drug company sales rep after a prescription has been pulled off the market. In the moment when the story breaks, your people don't know whether this is a minor or a major problem, and typically no one from corporate is going to speculate with them. As the media and online community respond (and perhaps overdramatize), the crisis inflates like a balloon, neighbors even ask about it over the backyard fence, and many of your people wonder whether they can survive the inevitable explosion. It is logical to have doubts and lose belief.

Perhaps you've witnessed this process firsthand: Initially during a challenge, employees are distracted by the possibilities of how the change will affect them. If left unaddressed, this gradually builds into a tsunami of worry. Workers become inert, and at that point many managers see the accelerating productivity slumps and start to panic, pouring fuel on the fire. Even if these setbacks are temporary, they can have lasting ramifications for a company's culture and the long-term confidence of employees.

One of the most important things that separates a great company from the pack is the way leaders respond to a loss of internal belief. Great cultures are prepared for these moments of crisis. Though no one can be ready for every disaster, great managers and organizations remain nimble enough to negotiate the treacherous path of reclaiming their reputation externally and the faith of their employees internally. If they can acknowledge the fears of workers and regain their trust first, the cumulative power can accelerate the return to normalcy for clients, customers, and shareholders. Furthermore, the proper management of an emergency assures employees that their belief in leadership is well founded and often creates a level of trust that is higher than before the crisis. Even dramatic setbacks need not have damaging permanent consequences if leaders acknowledge the problems, openly work to address the slump in morale, and apply the insights from our seven-step road map.

One of the most common crises we encounter is the appointment of a new leader. It can be especially taxing on employees as well as outside stakeholders—just consider the retirement and then passing of Apple CEO Steve Jobs or the precipitous drop in Hewlett-Packard's stock price after Mark Hurd's departure. Such a transition is bound to send shock waves throughout the system. New leadership must rapidly establish the processes and channels to communicate that things are under control in the business and plans are in place to manage an orderly succession.

The worst thing that can happen is that key stakeholders perceive new leadership to be in disarray, indecisive, or indifferent. Adherence to the process we outlined in this book is a powerful way to generate both the internal and external buy-in needed when a new leader takes over.

Consider, for instance, the case of one new manager and a soccer franchise that had lost its way.

≈ ALL IN ≈

REAL TURNAROUND

Soccer has been the next big thing in American sports for decades. On paper it looks like an obvious winner: One would think that the United States would be an ideal place to develop a league playing the world's most popular sport. After all, there is an immigrant population who grew up playing and loving the game, it's a sport that is easy to learn with few barriers of entry for young players (who don't have to be particularly big, fast, or coordinated to get started), it's equally welcoming to boys and girls, the equipment is cheap, it inspires rabid fans, there are midsized cities around the United States that crave professional sports teams, it's a sport whose World Cup tournaments stop the world's population in its tracks . . . We could go on, of course.

But for years soccer had been a disaster in the U.S. from a business viewpoint. In the last fifty years, leagues have sprung up around the country and then collapsed. It's been a painful evolution, full of turmoil and confounding organizational missteps. The following is a dizzying list of soccer leagues from the last few decades alone: the American Soccer League, International Soccer League, United Soccer Association, National Professional Soccer League, North American Soccer League, Western Soccer League, Lone Star Soccer Alliance, American Indoor Soccer Association, American Soccer League II, Major Indoor Soccer League, United Soccer Leagues, American Soccer League III, American Professional Soccer League, Sunbelt Independent Soccer League, United States Interregional Soccer League, and finally, Major League Soccer.

No kidding.

It was almost as though the sport were training the public to doubt its viability.

As for Major League Soccer, it was hemorrhaging money at its outset. *Businessweek* reported that this latest of leagues lost more than $350 million from the time of its founding in 1993 to 2004. And yet things were changing. Though it took some time to show up in revenues, the tide had started to turn following the 2002 World Cup, when the U.S. men's team made it to the quarterfinals. The nation was riveted by the quality of these mostly unknown American players—many of whom had been playing overseas at the time.

Major League Soccer took advantage of that momentum, with league officials devising a strategic plan that emphasized fiscal responsibility, including caps on team salaries. They also created reserve teams, like baseball's farm teams, to focus more attention on developing great American players than on importing them from abroad.

Fans started attending in much larger numbers, and they also started following their favorite teams online, making for lucrative ad revenue. Television networks signed contracts to air games and more and more advertisers began to express interest. Today marquee players like David Beckham and Thierry Henry draw huge crowds wherever they play, and cities are clamoring to join the league—some have even constructed beautiful, appropriately sized stadiums specifically for soccer. And some franchises are actually paying a profit to their owners.

The turnaround for U.S. soccer has been hard won, and one of the most startling turnaround stories has been in the mountain state of Utah, with a franchise named after one of the most successful football clubs in Spain, Real Madrid (pronounced *ray-al*—a Spanish word for "royal"). The two teams are not officially connected, although they have played an exhibition match in Utah.

Founded in 2004, Real Salt Lake had started with a bang and expectations were high. Attendance the first year was among the highest in the league, but by the time Bill Manning assumed his role as president in April 2008, the franchise had lost momentum and many in the front office had what he called a blasé attitude. "The team had a losing record and we were in a small market," says Manning. "Many seemed to think, *There's not much we can do.*"

The story of how the club started to thrive is a study in how a new management team can focus on culture, reigniting performance and growth. As proof, over the past three years Real Salt Lake has quadrupled sponsorship revenues and doubled season ticket sales, outcomes any business would be envious of.

The change was put in motion by the team's owner, Dave Checketts, who hired Manning and tasked him with achieving a transition. Manning was coming off a stint as vice president of sales and service for the Philadelphia Eagles of the National Football League. Under his leadership the Eagles saw a 50 percent increase in corporate sponsorships from the 2004 to 2007 seasons—leading *Forbes* magazine to cite the Eagles as the fastest-growing brand in the NFL.

With that impressive background, Manning could see the right ingredients were not in place for Real Salt Lake to take off, and he saw culture as a key factor: "We had to improve our staff, we had to improve our team on the field, and we had to change the culture. We needed an attitude of 'Do anything you can to win a big sponsorship or treat a customer to a great experience.'" For him, belief was crucial: "We had to build believers. We had to challenge people to work harder, be more efficient, and raise their game to another level."

The first step for the new president was to figure out who was with him and who was not.

Says Manning, when he takes on a new role he uses the formula of 25/50/25. He assumes that 25 percent of employees and managers will back him because he's the boss. These folks will be firmly in his corner and will need little more than a gentle nudge to keep them pointed in the right direction. Another 50 percent will be on the fence—waiting to see his full plan and see him in action before committing. Manning knows he can win them over if he shows that he cares and if he's wise with decisions. Then there are about 25 percent of people who will be resistant to a new leader, no matter how caring he is or what a track record of success he's had. At Real Salt Lake, he needed to move quickly and aggressively to get these people on board or move them out.

Howard Schultz faced a similar challenge when he reassumed the reins at Starbucks in January of 2008 after an eight-year absence. He was boldly direct with his leadership team, gathering them together and saying, "If you don't believe we can turn this company around, if you even have a smallest bit of doubt, come and see me privately. It will be easier to have this conversation now than if I have to come and find you three months from now. You have to really believe we can do this." Within a few months, Schultz told us, all but a few of those leaders were gone.

Said the Starbucks CEO of leading a turnaround, "Be honest and truthful, inspire hope and understanding, but above all be decisive."

As for Manning, early on he learned he had a battle on his hands in human resources. During the first few weeks he flew to a competing MLS franchise to study their way of doing business. While he was gone, a manager in HR approached his assistant and demanded to know where Manning was. When told he was traveling on business, the HR person insisted that if he wasn't there, he needed to take a vacation day and fill out a form. "I'm the president of the company, but we were rules-driven," says Manning. "If you weren't there, you must be on vacation.

"I can't tell you today where my senior vice presidents are right now, but I know they are doing good somewhere. That's how we needed to do business, with trust, with a focus on results, not worrying about who was filling up their chairs."

It was obvious that this HR person had little confidence in Manning. In our experience many people like this feel threatened by new leadership; perhaps their skills are not up-to-date. Others have developed a sense of entitlement because they have contributed to the company's success up to that point and can't see any need to change or head in a new direction. Despite frank conversations and coaching from Manning, the HR manager continued to undermine his leadership and was one of several people who had to be let go.

This process of evaluating his team was the beginning of establishing clear accountability, which he did throughout the organization. He made it clear that he expected people at all levels to step up. One night, a few weeks before the grand opening of the club's brand-new stadium, he sent an e-mail to his entire staff at 6:45 P.M. His note was simple: "Why is my car the only one in the parking lot three weeks before the stadium opener? Am I missing something?"

It was jarring, a bit brutal, and it was a wake-up call. The team was just weeks away from the grand opening of a $110 million building, and Manning was letting them know they would be standing on the edge of a burning platform very soon if they didn't start putting butts in seats.

The president also injected a new customer focus into the internal team's approach. That meant more emphasis on earning renewals of season tickets and creating deeper, more beneficial relationships with companies that might become sponsors. "The staff had spent a lot of time on selling but not on service," Manning explains. "Renewals on season tickets and sponsorships were very low, about sixty percent. The companies that are best, they put people on a conveyor belt and keep them on. Our renewal rate on sponsorships is now ninety-eight percent, and season ticket renewals are at eighty-six percent. That is millions of dollars in renewed revenue every year."

Manning emphasizes that all of those interacting with fans have to be serious about creating a positive memory for each guest, and again, he holds people accountable for doing so. "Our director of event services, Trino Martinez, spends a lot of time helping our concession workers, security personnel, and ticket takers understand how we want them to act when people come into our building," Manning explains. "Expectations are clear, even though these folks only work for us twenty games a year: We have a smile on our face, we greet people. If someone has a problem, each of us takes ownership."

Says Patti Benson, director of premium seating, "We ask our employees to think, 'What would you do if you had a party at your house? Wouldn't you do just about anything to make your guest feel comfortable? Now do that here.'"

Benson says that means encouraging every worker to get to know their customers' names, their spouses' names, their children's names. "We even learn their dogs' names. If their mother passes away, we go to the funeral. We form a strong bond."

On a typical Saturday evening at a Real Salt Lake match, if you ask where a certain gate is, it's not uncommon to have one of these temporary employees walk you there, asking along the way if it's your first game and what you think of the team's chances that night.

Manning also tapped into the extraordinary power of recognition, instituting a customer service award that he presents at every one of his all-hands meetings. In selecting winners, he considers feedback from fans, vendors, sponsors, and other employees, and then publically awards the winner a $250 Nordstrom gift card, since in his mind the retailer epitomizes outstanding service. "It may not be in someone's nature to be the best at customer service," he says, "but they want to win that award. They want me to call them up in front of all their peers and tell a story about their customer service exploits."

That first award was so effective that Manning added a second award, aimed at encouraging employees to root for each other, which he calls the Employee Appreciation Award. After presenting the Nordstrom gift card in a meeting, Manning now randomly calls on an employee and asks them whom they would like to recognize—which coincidentally ensures that no one ever nods off in these meetings.

Says Benson, "The customer service award usually goes to an employee in the box office or sales staff who treated a customer well. The Employee Appreciation Award goes to those who treat each other well—internally." This adept management approach has encouraged employees to care about not only fans and sponsors but also each other. It is recognition done right.

Let us tell you about one of these presentations.

A great believer in a "share everything" culture, Manning gathers his entire full-time staff regularly. In this particular meeting, the staff was going through the business of running the team and stadium: ticket sales, sponsorships, and an upcoming concert by rock legends Kiss that would be held at the stadium. "We'll need extra hairspray on hand," someone joked. At the end of the meeting Manning got ready to present the Employee Appreciation Award. They all knew they might be called on at random, so they were all ready with a name and story of another person on the team who deserved a $250 gift certificate to Best Buy.

Manning picked on an employee, John Kimball, who stood up and said, "You know, I've thought a lot about this. I think Devin Barlow [a bookkeeper] deserves this award. If you know anything about accounting in most companies, they are typically pretty hard to do business with—a black hole." More than a few heads were nodding at this point. "But our accounting group is the hub of our operation. Devin deals with all of us—ticket sales, sponsorship guys, merchandise, the camps. Thanks to Devin, the money comes in and goes out.

"He doesn't deal with a lot of customers, but whenever any one of us deals with Devin they walk away with a smile on their face. Sales is a stressful job, but when we feel good about the support we are getting we sell better. Without Devin we aren't selling."

The entire team applauded as Manning invited Barlow up on the stage. The young man was a bit shy but was grinning. On the way up he got a few high fives from his colleagues, and on the stage Manning presented him with the award and a warm handshake. With a level of deadpan only a bookkeeper could muster, Barlow said, "An accountant getting an award. I guess there is a snowball in hell."

Now, think about what happened here and how it relates to the STEP formula we presented earlier. John, a senior member of the staff, told a *story* about Devin in front of the entire team, which had been gathered *together*. He *emphasized* what matters most to the organization—not only external service but internal. And finally, he *personalized* the moment by talking about Devin's characteristics—that he gets invoices to clients on time, that he's a joy to work with, that he tackles problems with a willing attitude. It's a near-perfect example of "rooting for each other" in action, and President Manning did very little except call on someone.

Now, how would this have happened in most organizations? At best, the president would have heard good things about Devin; perhaps he would have called him into his office and given him an award or a little extra in his paycheck. But Manning didn't. Why? Because Devin already knew that what he was doing was great. The award ceremony was to let others know and to teach all sixty-two people the value of serving each other. Don't you think each of these team members wanted to perform similar heroics after witnessing this presentation?

Manning says, "I want everyone to walk into our meetings engaged and thinking about who they appreciate. It makes you think about who you like working with, and that's one way you build an energized culture."

Another way is with day-to-day recognition, quick spot awards at the team level. After each game, the team's director of merchandising, Brett Fischer, gathers all forty of his full- and part-time employees and presents his award for the All-Star of the Match. "We look for those who went above and beyond, who did something unique," says Fischer. "Last game it was Kirk Jensen. We call him Captain Kirk now, because he had a vision to increase activity in one area of our merchandising and he took sales from a thousand dollars a night to five thousand dollars. We gave him a round of applause and presented him with a jersey he'd been wanting."

Manning also brought a new consciousness about serving customers to the task of increasing sponsorships. "A few years ago our sponsors felt like they were doing us a favor by spending ten thousand dollars with us, and they probably were at the time," says the president. "I told our staff that if we want to be major league we need to enhance the value of who we are. That meant giving these clients better value, exposure, and care."

But the stakes got much higher in the fall of 2008, as Real Salt Lake came close to completing its new stadium in Sandy, Utah, a suburb of Salt Lake City, and looked to sign a sponsor to put its name on the building—a potential multiyear, multimillion-dollar contract.

"No one thought we would sell the naming rights," Manning says. "And the way we were going we probably wouldn't have. A marketing firm hired before I came on board was explaining to potential clients that it would be a privilege to have a soccer stadium named after them. In the old days we thought companies should do business with us because we play soccer games or football or basketball, but you've got to step outside your comfort zone and be creative. We let that firm go and took over ourselves. We started to think about what potential sponsors needed."

A local copper mine came onto the radar for the sales staff. As one of the largest employers in the area, the mine would benefit from a positive community presence. The company had also recently changed its name from Kennecott Copper to Rio Tinto, and a naming-rights deal could increase name recognition for the new brand.

Team owner Checketts and Manning invited the mine's top brass to a tour of the new stadium well before completion, while it still resembled an Erector Set of girders and beams. Construction workers, staff, and even players greeted the mine's executives wearing hard hats and polo shirts with a new Rio Tinto Stadium logo they had designed. Everywhere the mine bosses went, bold signage proclaimed the potential partnership.

As a minerals company, Rio Tinto was very cognizant of environmental issues and safety, so Manning pointed out the green aspects of the structure as well as how they cared about the well-being of the crews at work.

But it was a viewing area that got the most attention. Manning had borrowed a powerful telescope from the University of Utah and placed it high in the stadium where the executives could get a glimpse of the Rio Tinto mine to the west. "The CEO looked into the telescope, saw the mine, and said, 'Wow, maybe we can put a Real Salt Lake flag in the mine that people can identify.'" Manning almost pulled out a contract right then.

"We did our homework. We knew it was important to them that the people of Utah feel Rio Tinto is an important part of the community. So we explained how Real Salt Lake would come into communities and do clinics where the mine is located and how those kids would come out to their stadium and watch a professional game."

During this entire first meeting, Manning and his staff didn't put a dollar figure on a potential agreement. They instead talked about a connection between a company and a community. "It was about emotion," he says. "We wanted to show that people will have a favorable image of Rio Tinto because they came here and enjoyed themselves."

Two days later the mine's external relations director, Gina Crezee, called back. She admitted the executives had come on the tour simply as a favor to Checketts and had been emphatic beforehand that they would decline the naming-rights deal. But she said, "I'm happy to tell you we would like to engage in further discussion."

During that due diligence period, the value Manning had placed on consistent customer-focus contributed to sealing the deal. Crezee was at a soccer tournament with her son while the company was still undergoing its evaluation, and with no idea who the mine executive was, Real Salt Lake star forward Yura Movsisyan kicked the ball around with her child. What's more, when the little boy asked for an autograph, the footballer signed his forehead with a marker. Mom and son were in heaven, and when they got home the boy refused to wash for days. The culture was spreading.

Says Manning, "It was a little thing, but it showed the quality and character of the players and staff. Gina said, 'Wow, if he's a representative of Real Salt Lake, then he's a representative of Rio Tinto.'"

Within a few weeks, the mine signed a ten-year contract, the largest sponsorship by far in the team's history and one of the most lucrative ever in Major League Soccer. It was a turning point in the progression of Real Salt Lake, and there were few unbelievers left on the staff.

"Our staff and team were starting to learn that no matter if it's the CEO of a sponsor or a fan who buys two south-goal tickets once a year, we want to give people a memory every time they come into contact with us."

The results have been exceptional. When Manning came on board in 2008, the team was earning about $1.5 million a year in sponsorship revenue; it's now $7 million. Season ticket sales have grown from 4,000 to 8,000, with more than 17,000 people showing up for most games, which is near tops for the league despite the fact that Real Salt Lake is in one of the smallest markets.

The team on the field started to believe as well. Real Salt Lake started to win just as big. In 2009, the underdog, overlooked team from one of the league's smallest markets won game after game in the postseason, finally matching up in the MLS Cup final with the star-studded Los Angeles Galaxy, fielding superstars David Beckham and Landon Donovan. After a regulation-time 1-1 draw and a goalless overtime, Robbie Russell scored in the seventh round of penalty kicks to give Real Salt Lake its first-ever Major League Soccer championship.

On a freezing evening in late November, tens of thousands of cheering fans lined State Street in Salt Lake City as players and staff drove by hoisting the cup.

Manning and his front office have assembled an impressive group of players on the field and off. And despite that championship and the team's unprecedented 2011 run to the CONCACAF finals (missing by one goal a chance to represent North and Central America against Barcelona and other elite teams in the FIFA Club World Cup), Manning still pushes his staff. And in turn they now know that nothing is insurmountable.

"In 2007 our people had lost the belief that they were part of something great," he says. "We've stopped the free fall and we are climbing again. The easy part is getting to the top of the mountain; the hard part is to stay there, to sustain momentum and growth. We still don't have a sold-out building every game, we want our team to compete for a championship every year, and there are still season tickets to sell and customers to wow. There are always new challenges ahead."

We will give the last word on Real Salt Lake to founder and chairman Dave Checketts, who told us, "Our executive leadership group of Bill, Garth [Lagerwey], and Jason [Kreis] established a culture that took our vision of management to the highest levels. It has allowed us to stand out as a model franchise in MLS and along the way become a true community asset—achievements I am very proud of."

Some of you right now may feel the challenge in front of you is insurmountable, that it is not in your power to change an entire culture or influence a transformation of financial results with the very real challenges you face. But renewal can and does occur, and as we've shown, it can happen quickly when the right leader follows the right path. Adherence to the seven-step road map we have presented is the simplest way to generate internal buy-in and overcome resistance. Whether you run a small team or a large corporation you can follow this process to dramatically increase the odds of building a culture that will last.

12

Fifty-two Ways to Get Your People All In

Most new leaders are chosen by those at the top of the organizational chart, but true leadership doesn't come with the knightly dubbed bestowal of an important-sounding title; it grows organically based on character, competency, trust, and a hint of humanity and fun thrown in for good measure. Real leaders are able to inspire belief in their cause and in themselves. And since developing a culture is a journey, below we offer fifty-two ways to keep the momentum going. These ideas are in no particular order. Some might work in your organization and some might not, but try one a week and see if belief grows.

1. Ask a billion questions. Thought-provoking questions not only open the lines of communication but also allow employees to view their potential and reach for it. A few starters: Is the job what you expected? What skills do you have that we aren't using? What's the best thing that's happened to you this week? Do you understand how your job fits into the company strategy? What aspects of your job do you find frustrating? Are you getting all the information you need to do your job effectively? What could we do to have more fun around here?

Belief Challenge: Add a lot more question marks to your daily conversations. Valuing others' opinions builds trust and allows employees to form their own opinions, which hopefully will one day coincide with yours.

2. Balance the time budget. Effective managers in industries from high tech to manufacturing create visual representations of employee workloads—allowing them to more accurately track bandwidth. When a leader and an employee collaboratively agree to put an assignment on these charts ahead of something else, the expectation is very clear. It's also easier to postpone or eliminate low-priority projects when you can clearly see that an employee's entire month is already booked solid. We refer to this practice as balancing the time budget, which is just as important as balancing your other work budgets.

Belief Challenge: Ask yourself: Do you help each employee prioritize his or her assignments on a regular basis?

3. Be a part-timer lover. The Fulham Football Club of the English Premier League has a thousand occasional workers who take tickets, manage crowd control, and sell refreshments during the team's home games. They call these employees "those on the edges," and Robert Ordever, people-development director, says, "They have far more influence over our success or failure than anything management can do in the head office. Those on the edges are our front face, our ambassadors, our brand, and our best source of feedback from our fans and customers." To build understanding, the club invests more time educating these part-timers than they do training their full-time staff. Leaders also ensure each occasional worker feels empowered to take action to do what is necessary to create an exceptional fan experience, and when they go above and beyond, they're recognized. The result, says Ordever, "is a real improvement in the quality of service offered to [their] fans." "Our values are not simply a poster, but are lived and breathed," Ordever explains. "We continue to get increased numbers of customer commendations and we have grown our attendance numbers in difficult and highly competitive times."

Belief Challenge: Ask yourself: Have we fully trained our part-timers?

4. Make small commitments. Hold a Monday staff meeting where each member of your team—including you—defines a stretch goal that can be achieved by week's end. Post the goals on a whiteboard or intranet site. Then follow up with a Thursday afternoon meeting where employees report on their status. Something about the combination of setting their own goals and doing it in front of their peers brings out the best in team members.

Belief Challenge: When was the last time you held yourself accountable for hitting a goal in front of your employees?

5. End the week with thanks. Every Friday, celebrate what the team has achieved during the week. Don't forget to highlight the individual contributions of outstanding employees. Then channel the energy that is created to set goals for the following week.

Belief Challenge: How long has it been since you celebrated a team or individual accomplishment in public? (If it's been longer than a week, you aren't doing all you can to build your culture.)

6. I do declare. At Tastefully Simple, the warehouse team supports more than 23,000 direct-sales consultants across the United States. It's an important behind-the-scenes job, so the entire team got together recently to think about how they wanted to act. Table activities and a group discussion generated the Warehouse Community Declaration, which was signed by every person. Each team member received a copy, rolled up like a scroll, and the original was framed and posted for everyone to see—it's also reviewed with every new warehouse team member as part of orientation. The declaration includes ideas such as "Our work has special meaning and we intend to act that way," "The customer pays good money for the Tastefully Simple products they purchase. It's up to us to get that product to them in perfect condition," and "We will have fun at work." (The entire document is posted at TheCultureWorks.com.)

Belief Challenge: Can you give your employees a voice in writing your own team declaration?

7. Start the day on a high. Avis Budget Group posts upbeat renter letters in its online mailbox. While they are always eager to learn from problems that arise, they only feature compliments in morning e-mails to their locations. The theory is to kick each day off with a positive. One rental center manager achieves similar results by blasting wake-up music for staff members who arrive in the early-morning hours.

Belief Challenge: What can you do to help start tomorrow on a high note?

8. Believe in yourself. The best thing you can do for your team is to believe in your own and your team's collective goals. In his autobiography, legendary runner Roger Bannister admitted that there were other runners who were faster than he was, but he was the first to truly *believe* he could break a four-minute mile. That belief, he said, made all the difference.

Belief Challenge: How can you demonstrate to employees that you believe in them and in your collective team goals?

9. Care. We had a meeting delayed recently, but the executive we were to meet with texted us to say she was running late. "With my employee Kat who is in the hospital. Be there in 10," was the message. We shot back, "How kind of you!" She replied, "Wouldn't any manager do the same?" When she put it that way, the answer was clear. Of course, any leader worth following would care enough about a sick or injured employee to visit them in the hospital, but the sad truth is that the majority don't care. Be the exception.

Belief Challenge: If asked, do you attend your employees' weddings, funerals, parties, or other important life events?

10. Talk the walk. Spread belief in your goals by talking as if success is guaranteed. Replace "if" with "when"—then switch out "try" for "will." Your enthusiasm will be contagious. As we found, Michael Phelps had a near-perfect swimmer's body and highly developed technique, but it wasn't until he started to believe he could win eight Olympic races that it became possible.

Belief Challenge: Think back to your last conversation with your team. Did you use fatalistic language, or did you assume success?

11. Answer them. Think *your* in-box is full? Frank Martire, president and chief executive officer of FIS, one of the largest banking technology firms in the United States, with 32,000 employees, personally responds to every single one of the thousands of employee questions he gets as part of the "Ask the CEO" initiative. Most contain tactical questions, but there are unusual requests, like the one from the San Antonio office that wanted an ice machine (which Martire helped them secure). The initiative has continued for eight years. Said Lisa Sweeney, FIS VP of employee engagement, "Frank communicates what is important to all of us on a daily basis. The other leaders take the cue from Frank. Our entire executive team is extremely committed to driving employee engagement, to living our guiding principles, and that comes from Frank's leadership, but we also believe it."

Belief Challenge: Do you respond to every employee e-mail the same day, even if it's a simple "Let me get back with you on that, and please don't let me forget"?

12. A week of gratitude. In employees' minds, a paycheck is the fulfillment of a contract; it's expected. What is rare and unexpected is gratitude. Surprise employees with an Employee Appreciation Week where their contributions are acknowledged and celebrated every day in unique ways.

Belief Challenge: Could you come up with five unique ways of thanking employees next week?

13. A hero's quest. Sir Galahad's quest to find the Holy Grail required an epic journey and sacrifice. In business, tackling big challenges is akin to a quest—it takes considerable time and effort to achieve your goal, something most work groups just aren't willing to invest. But twice a year, Equitable Life and Casualty brings together a group of at least thirty employees to undertake what they call Quest events. The teams tackle problems and ideas in all areas of the company that deal with day-to-day operations. And once a year, the company also puts together four or five teams with five or six people that look at competition, new product possibilities, best-in-class companies, technology, and better ways to serve their agents and consumers.

Belief Challenge: What thorny issues could an employee team tackle in your organization?

14. The five-year rule. When employee goals align with organizational goals, magic happens. That's why, in his first meeting with employees, Scott O'Neil, president of Madison Square Garden in New York City, asks, "Where do you want to be five years from now?" He commits to helping each employee get there if they'll commit to giving their very best every day. Who wouldn't be all in with such a promise from their leader?

Belief Challenge: Do you know the goals and aspirations of each of your employees? Are they written down?

15. Send an HTN. Computers can do almost everything these days—some are so advanced they only require *four reboots* after an error alert—but nothing produced by machine can equal the power of a handwritten thank-you note (HTN)—even if you use a cursive-style font. People hang HTNs on their cubicle walls and save them for years. If you don't have a stack of cards ready to use, get some and send out at least three every week.

Belief Challenge: How many thank-you notes did you send out last month to people who helped you—employees, coworkers, vendors, clients, etc.? If it's less than ten, it's time to pick up the pace.

16. Perk your products. When employees truly love the products or services they provide, it shows. At the Atlantis Resort at Paradise Island in the Bahamas, employees regularly receive hotel stays and get to swim with the dolphins. Besides making them feel valued, this allows employees to experience resort benefits from the customer's perspective, helping them to better serve their clients.

Belief Challenge: What employee perk could you offer that would allow employees to use your products?

17. Create a vision for the future. For almost sixty years, Ability Beyond Disability has helped people with disabilities pursue lives that most of us take for granted, finding them homes, training them to work, helping them find jobs, and above all teaching people the skills to make friends, pursue their interests, and feel good about themselves. Anticipating exponential growth in the number people with disabilities, the organization recently made it its goal to double the number of people it can serve and put together a "vision for the future." This vision document came after months of research and interviews with members of the community, employees, and the board of directors.

Belief Challenge: Can you talk with your stakeholders and collaboratively put together a pathway forward for your team?

18. Play like a team. It turns out that the old-school company softball teams were more than just fun and games and beer-fueled melees. In the best cultures, colleagues find ways to pull together as a team outside of work, building pride in the organization and developing stronger interpersonal relationships. Ragnar Relays are all the rage for groups looking to build camaraderie, but bowling, golf, a Facebook community, and even laser tag are fun too. Regardless of the activity, the benefits of being a team outside of work remain the same—increased communication and group identity.

Belief Challenge: When was the last time your entire team did something outside of the workplace?

19. Find other believers. Successful leaders surround themselves with mentors and friends who share ambitious goals—and believe they are attainable. When James H. Maynard, founder of Golden Corral, needed a loan to open his first restaurant, and no bank would lend him the money, he turned to his friends. Started in 1972, the Golden Corral chain now includes more than 500 restaurants and employs more than 9,000 people. That's the power of friendship (not to mention all-you-can-eat buffets!).

Belief Challenge: Do you spend time with other businesspeople who uplift you or those who bring your spirits down?

20. Lighten up. All work meetings don't have to be PowerPoint slides and yawn-inducing pie charts. Mix in a little fun with the work. Insert a Dilbert comic or something lighthearted. You still get the work done, but everyone enjoys it much more. Innocent, a UK company with a focus on making "tasty little drinks," has this concept down pat. Each year, prior to the company meeting, employees are asked, "What would you do with $1,000?" The question isn't hypothetical; at the company meeting, the top five finalists (selected by the management team) have five minutes to pitch their dreams to the crowd. A crowd vote determines who gets the $1,000. Of course, fun doesn't have to cost a grand. We've seen a team act out an entire book of ours—a parable—in full costume during a senior leadership gathering. Other groups play Minute to Win It games at the start of their meetings to get people involved and thinking outside the box. Studies prove that laughter is a key factor in enhancing creativity.

Belief Challenge: What could you do to lighten up your next meeting?

21. Random recognition. Invite everyone to come to your next weekly meeting thinking of someone they appreciate—someone preferably working behind the scenes who doesn't get a lot of thanks. Then randomly at the end of the meeting ask an employee whom they appreciate, and then present the appreciated person with an award.

Belief Challenge: Could you implement random recognition in your staff meetings?

22. Adopt a symbol. Team or company symbols are a way to keep your mission and priorities in front of employees. The object itself can be anything that is meaningful to your group—we've seen teams adopt a compass, eagle, or rowing team—even a monkey, rubber chicken, big dog, or GI Joe doll. At the Pepsi Bottling Group, which we profiled earlier, a miniature brass Pepsi delivery truck, given to employees who lived the Pepsi "rules of the road," became one of the organization's most coveted awards.

Belief Challenge: Does your team have a symbol or mascot that employees could rally around?

23. A thirty-minute miracle. Jason was new at his job and met a man named Jeff, who always seemed to find a few minutes to talk each day. A few days later Jason was shocked to learn that Jeff was a very busy, very successful director. "My first reaction was disbelief," Jason said. "My next was to be impressed that he could be in such a high-profile job and still be a real, everyday kind of guy who cared enough to connect with us." Is spending thirty or sixty minutes a day talking to the people who work for you a waste of time? Not if it enables you to develop deeper, trusting, real relationships. At Texas Health Presbyterian Hospital Dallas, president Britt Berrett and his entire staff leave their offices every day at 9:00 A.M. to connect with teammates. It's brought staff and management closer together and is facilitating real improvements.

Belief Challenge: Can you commit to spending just thirty minutes a day "making the rounds" and talking with employees?

24. Seriously? The funny thing about leadership is, the more you try to seem important, the sillier you become to employees who are turned off by your self-importance. Fun goes a long way toward bringing a team together. At Zappos.com, leaders have dance-offs on a regular basis, and they are the most attended meetings at the online retailer's headquarters. The idea is make a fool of yourself and let everyone know that, as leaders, you don't take yourselves too seriously.

Belief Challenge: Are you too grim? Ask a few employees for their candid comments.

25. Pimp your titles. All the "specialists" and "coordinators" of the world, unite. For good or bad, and to varying degrees, people define themselves by their titles, so why not create one that they love? At Pixar all employees are called filmmakers—whether they work as a night watchman, receptionist, or animator. And if you work at Pixar and have a child born during the making of a movie, they get a credit too in the "Production Babies" list. People have been known to induce labor for such an honor.

Belief Challenge: Is it possible to give your people the right to choose their own creative titles? "Vice president" and "director" might be out for political reasons, but who says they can't be the "guru of all things logistical" or the "mayor of manufacturing"?

26. Get healthy. Some organizations have started giving their employees thirty minutes a day for exercise, and we're not talking, "Johnson, drop and give me twenty for your insolence!" Zions Bancorporation deposits money into employee health savings accounts when they complete health challenges. And Cigna encourages employees to take the stairs by posting artwork created by employees' children in the stairwells. Other companies have installed blood-pressure machines, offer flu shots at the workplace, or bring medical personnel to their location to provide annual employee physicals.

Belief Challenge: What can you do to positively affect the health of your team members?

27. The good stuff. It's amazing how much employees can learn about your commitment to them just from the T-shirt you hand out at the annual employee party. We visited one television news network where an employee complained that management makes them wear "cheap knockoffs" of the real logoed

polo shirts and ball caps. And yet at network CNN, employees receive the same high-quality gear that is sold in the retail stores. The message for employees is clear: "We value our staff."

Belief Challenge: Is there anything in your practices that might be making employees feel less valued?

28. The guessing game. Perhaps you've heard of parallel play—when children play alongside each other but never interact. Kids outgrow it, but some adults in the workplace get permanently stuck in a similar state we call parallel work. People in this state can be on the same team for years without ever really engaging with each other in meaningful ways (much like the U.S. Congress). This lack of real interaction prevents the team from coalescing. Leaders can encourage teams to interact through activities like the one described by one of our workshop participants: "We have a large entrance wall that we inaugurated by having each employee post something about themselves that others wouldn't know. The first day we didn't put our name with our unique things, and we all tried to guess what belonged to whom. The person with the most correct won a prize. It got us talking and laughing and we learned a lot about the people in the cubicles next to us."

Belief Challenge: Do you have a wall or online space that could be used for a guessing game? Ask a trusted employee to help you organize a game for next week.

29. Personal milestones. Just as the best managers are there to help during employee difficulties, they also remember to celebrate positive employee milestones. Usually, this is as simple as giving a birthday card, attending a wedding, or sending a baby gift, but some go further. Some managers note the birthdays of employees' children (and pets to give equal time to those without children). They then give their people a little time off on these special days.

Belief Challenge: Get to know the birthdays of your employees and their children and make sure they leave early those days.

30. Good endings. People leave jobs. Even stars leave. Do all you can to avoid losing your most talented people, but if they go there's no point in getting upset. After all, people get better offers, spouses are transferred, there is an interesting opportunity in another field, employees go back to school, or they retire. Whatever the reason, the way you say good-bye speaks volumes about who you are as an organization and who you are as a leader. Remember, people can either become customers of your product and ambassadors of your brand or they can become your worst competitor. It is your choice.

Belief Challenge: Think about how you treated your last departing employee—like a valued partner whom you would like to work with again, or as a distraction and bother?

31. World record. People like to be part of something special. Then why not work hard to set your group or organization apart from the crowd? Pets at Home, the UK's largest pet store chain, recently sponsored the World's Biggest Dog Walk, setting a world record in the process—with more than 22,000 dogs and owners walking 3.5 miles. Imagine the goodwill that was created in the eyes of their customers (not to mention the job security for city sanitation workers).

Belief Challenge: Is there something your team could set out to accomplish with your customers that could set you apart and bring you all closer together? While you might not actually break a world record, it's sure fun trying.

32. Time out. Research shows that employees who take short breaks are more productive than those who work straight through the day. Plan an occasional pause to energize your staff. Activities don't have to be elaborate. It might be as simple as turning on some music and working together to keep a balloon in the air over your cubicle walls for five minutes (and trying to break your record over several days) or walking to a nearby coffee shop or juice bar together. Employee contests are also fun. One team we studied had a product quiz with winners getting donuts. LinkedIn invited team members to participate in a "Pimp My Cube" event. The company provided a small budget for decorations and employee themes ranged from Angry Birds to a beach luau to *Star Wars,* getting everyone to think creatively.

Belief Challenge: What can you do today to give people a creative break?

33. A tidal wave. Imagine showing up at the office to find not just one but a pile of HTNs (handwritten thank-you notes) from your colleagues expressing their gratitude for your contributions to the team. You'd probably keep the stack of notes for a long time and remember how you felt forever. Organizing a group tidal wave of appreciation is a fun way to remind behind-the-scenes team members that their efforts don't go unnoticed.

Belief Challenge: Is there someone who may be underappreciated on your team but always thinks of others? Organize a tidal wave for them today.

34. Get hands-on. Taking pride in your craft is important, whether you pour cement, audit company books, or play in a symphony orchestra. It's a manager's job to provide opportunities to rekindle their employees' passion for their craft. Stanley Hainsworth, a designer of great renown, told us about his team's annual Design Camps, which he calls "opportunities to spend time together, free of traditional work expectations, to be creatively inspired and bond with each other." Hainsworth says, "We bring in amazing people and activities that are designed to rejigger our creative minds and inspire us in new ways." And to inspire creativity and teamwork at his design agency, Tether, employees learn to work together using an old-fashioned letterpress machine. "The machine is cumbersome and slow, but it represents the craft and love of design. We have studio-wide letterpress projects where we can get hands-on designing something around a theme and then work alongside each other to create these."

Belief Challenge: In what ways could you inspire those around you to greater creative heights?

35. Don't miss the "previews." In addition to formal midyear and year-end performance reviews, Hainsworth holds monthly one-on-one "previews" that give him and his employees the chance to evaluate progress toward goals and make course corrections in between these bigger milestones. These don't need to take place in a formal work environment either. Take them out to lunch or hit a bucket of balls while chatting.

Belief Challenge: Are you sitting down one-on-one with your direct reports and their reports at least quarterly to check on their progress?

36. Let them write the check. Eli Lilly puts the power of philanthropy in employee hands. Employees worldwide can donate to more than 800 grassroots projects across the globe and have their donations matched by the Eli Lilly and Company Foundation. Employees may support hundreds of grassroots programs, including projects that improve the care of people with tuberculosis in India, teach farmers in Zambia about animal management and sustainable farming, or provide an education for orphaned children in Cameroon. And to encourage employees to participate in the new program, the Ely Lilly and Company Foundation in 2011 offered every eligible Lilly employee worldwide the opportunity to direct a $50 credit toward a cause that was most meaningful to them.

Belief Challenge: What can you do as a team to support a charity in your community?

37. Evaluation time. In their book *Difficult Conversations,* authors Douglas Stone, Bruce Patton, Sheila Heen, and Roger Fisher teach us that our self-worth hinges on our answers to three deceptively simple questions:

a. Am I competent?
b. Am I a good person?
c. Am I worthy of love?

Belief Challenge: It's worth a leader's time to ask if he is helping each of his employees answer these profound questions in the affirmative.

38. Serve. If you don't have a lot of money to invest in community involvement, get creative. A bank we visited in Idaho has a paint-a-thon, where employees clean, repair, and paint the exterior of low-income homes in disrepair. The manager's investment is minimal (paint, brushes, and food for the volunteers) but the impact on employee engagement, bank image, and the community is significant.

Belief Challenge: Can you take a few hours off this month to work together for the betterment of a charity?

39. Get ideas out of their pockets. Many employees might relate to the character Norm Peterson of *Cheers,* who said, "It's a dog-eat-dog world out there, and I'm wearing Milk-Bone underwear!" Your employees have more to give, especially ideas, but many feel insignificant and unheard in the corporate culture. Every organization should have a designated ombudsman who is accountable for listening to employees—not a boss, but a person who is tasked with evaluating employee ideas and, if they are viable, helping present them to management.

Belief Challenge: What can you do to better market your employees' ideas to those above and around you?

40. Who's driving? One way to ensure buy-in for your next initiative is to put employees in the driver's seat. Their fresh perspectives and ownership can be surprising and valuable. At one small firm we studied, employees were charged with determining the company's charitable giving platform. They dedicated a full two days where they put a hold on paying work and spent the time as teams coming up with how and where the company would donate its spare time and money.

Belief Challenge: How can you get your employees more

involved in key initiatives, perhaps getting them to own an important piece of them?

41. Taking turns as teacher. In staff meetings, some leaders invite team members to prepare and present short educational moments on the subject of their choice. Topics range from explanations of their team's corner of the intranet to reviews of new business books to instructions on how to use the department-owned camera or how to make a great red velvet cake. These teaching moments give team members practice in their craft, or something fun, and expand the group's knowledge base (not to mention their waistlines).

Belief Challenge: Can you add an educational minute in your staff meetings?

42. Share. As a manager, proactively sharing information that might be valuable to team members allows your team to make better decisions and increases members' confidence in each other. One employee shared a frustration with a boss he otherwise likes working for. "He keeps information from me—stuff that isn't confidential but that could help me. So I end up hearing important things from other people and I wonder . . . is it a power play?"

Belief Challenge: Are you open with your employees, sharing all you are able to as soon as you can?

43. Vive la différence. Every team starts out full of gaps—culture gaps, style gaps, generation gaps, experience gaps, education gaps, background gaps, and even language gaps. Rather than trying to erase these differences and create a team of clones, effective leaders try to understand and maximize individuality, creating an environment where different perspectives are welcomed and valued as advantages. Remember that a diverse team is more likely to innovate than a team full of people who think and act the same.

Belief Challenge: How can you encourage stronger diversity of ideas on your team?

44. The remains for the staff? Some people claim that Hard Rock Calling, the outdoor rock concert for charity hosted by Hard Rock Café in London every year, is the greatest party on earth. The event at Hyde Park draws top-drawer performers from around the world. But ask Hard Rock staff, and they'll tell you the real event is the after-party, thrown by the company for Hard Rock staff. Everything is first-class, no leftovers— and employees eat it up. More than half the photos posted online after the festivities are from the staff party. And leadership never has trouble recruiting employees for the following year's event.

Belief Challenge: Do you give your staff the best, or could they accuse you of giving them the leftovers?

45. Change a community. Capital One built a soccer-field park and a baseball diamond at its McLean, Virginia, headquarters and opened it up for employee and community use. Besides improving worker health, it provided needed community recreational space. Our friends at Murphy Oil in El Dorado, Arkansas, donated $50 million to fund college educations for all of the town's high school graduates. Any student who has lived in El Dorado for at least four years can get a full-ride scholarship. This generosity has changed the entire community. Not only are more than 95 percent of the high school graduates now going to college (up from 60 percent just a few years ago), but housing prices have risen 14 percent in a down economy.

Belief Challenge: What ideas does your team have to influence the community for the better?

46. Giving feedback. Because honest, constructive feedback is so difficult to give *and* receive, many leaders avoid it whenever possible. Great leaders, however, view feedback as an essential tool and have learned to hold up a mirror to employees in a way that motivates necessary leaps to higher performance levels. The key is perspective. When leaders are focused on the employee's success and not on themselves and their agendas, feedback usually moves away from destructive finger-pointing toward constructive communication, creating a trusting environment where uncomfortable subjects can be discussed.

Belief Challenge: Think about your last feedback session with an employee. Did you vent pent-up frustrations, or were you able to be direct while still keeping the employee's best interests at heart?

47. Speak to the heart. While many vision or mission statements devolve into a laundry list of activities and buzz words that no one can remember, Walt Disney's vision was just four words: "Dream. Believe. Dare. Do." Those words helped define a culture of creativity, intelligent risk-taking, and empowerment.

Belief Challenge: If you had to describe your team in just three or four words, what would they be? Now, what would you want them to be?

48. Lead by example. Gandhi said, "Be the change you want to see in the world." It's good advice for life and it's especially good for managers. Years ago we visited a hospital cafeteria after one of the busiest lunchtimes anyone could recall. Dishes and pots were stacked twenty deep all around the kitchen. Overwhelmed by the task in front of them, the employees appeared to be frozen, until the director of nutritional services stepped forward, rolled up his sleeves, filled a sink with water, and got to work. The boss's example inspired everyone else to follow suit.

Belief Challenge: When faced with a software failure, production slowdown, or major customer issue, do you roll up your sleeves and help out?

49. Hire trust. It's relatively easy to teach a candidate your business. What can't be taught is trustworthiness. Sure, your usual background check will expose things like prison terms or perhaps fines for "testing" too many grapes at a grocery store, but a lot can and does slip through the filter. The following interview questions may help you better gauge a candidate's trust level:

- Tell me about a time when you were asked to compromise your values, and why you made the choice you did.
- What values did your parents or other mentors teach you?
- What would you do if your best friend did something illegal?

Belief Challenge: Think about your own interviewing style. How many questions do you ask that gauge a candidate's honesty and trustworthiness?

50. Watch for the assists. A leader we met recently at a fast-driving investment firm added "assisting team members" as a goal in employee performance reviews. "Universally, everyone expressed surprise at the notion that helping each other was worthy of inclusion on an appraisal," he said. "They actually fought it, and that told me something about the culture I had created. Our culture was about looking out for yourself and not your teammates." That had to change.

Belief Challenge: What kind of incentive or accountability tool could you offer to ensure better teamwork in your work group?

51. Encourage cheer. Pret a Manger (French for "ready to eat") has a sales growth rate that's through the roof. Their difference? Fast food with smiles—genuine, sincere, how-are-you-doing kind of happiness in places like frenzied midtown Manhattan and central London. The company's goal is to serve customers in a friendly manner within sixty seconds—even at peak times in their shops—and that takes a concerted amount of teamwork. At Pret a Manger, executives say, the solution to better teamwork is to hire, pay, and promote based on—believe it or not—qualities like cheerfulness.

Belief Challenge: How can you encourage cheerfulness on your team?

52. Build trust. Today in the United States 55 percent of people believe that companies will take advantage of the public if they think they can get away with it. Trust is on the decline in all aspects of American life, and we all need to act. The first step? Lose the jargon. After all, if I don't understand you, I won't trust you. Second, keep your promises. Reward employees who own problems and see issues through to resolution. And third, lift up your trustworthy heroes as examples. When people act in a way that builds confidence, communicate their actions publicly and, of course, reward their behavior.

Belief Challenge: When was the last time you held up an example of trustworthiness?

13

In the Company of Believers

A Wealth of Rewards

L ate in the fifteenth century, a burly, white-haired Genoese trader arrived in the court of Spain with a far-fetched
scheme, to set sail west into uncharted waters and discover a
new route to Asia. All he needed was a small fortune to outfit an
armada of vessels capable of crossing the immense ocean. It was
a request that was met with considerable derision by most in the
court of King Ferdinand and Queen Isabella. The country was
near bankruptcy, the trader had never sailed farther than North
Africa, and, most overwhelming, many of the country's learned
citizens assumed the Atlantic and Pacific oceans to be connected
with no land between, much too vast for any ship to cross.

The sailor, intelligent and ambitious, realized he had to fash-
ion a radically new culture with these potential investors, and
so in their first meeting he laid before the Spanish queen a map
of the world. The chart, which he and his brother had prepared,
showed the ocean, in his estimate, to be wide but navigable. He
threw his arms apart as he mused on the riches the court would
garner from opening a new way to the East. And, knowing his
audience well, the crafty trader spoke at length to the devout
Isabella of carrying the Gospel of Christ to the far reaches of the
earth, quoting ample scripture to make his point.

Isabella didn't say yes, but she also didn't say no. She was
more than a little intrigued and asked that the merchant argue his

case before a committee of learned men. He did so, but also spent considerable time persuading and placating others in the court, even down to the reclusive bursars who controlled the purse strings. Weeks, months, and years passed, and while some men might have sought a compromise to put an end to the scrutiny, the trader realized he needed to become bolder. He argued that he should be named governor-general of the new lands he would claim and an admiral of the Spanish navy, and he even requested a tenth of all new riches as his own. It was actually a shrewd tactical maneuver. The request took the idea from fancy into the realm of reality. He was painting a picture that the expedition would indeed win new territory and secure untold fortunes; the only question, it seemed, was how they would be distributed.

It was a brilliant plan, patiently and strategically executed. And finally Isabella and Ferdinand made their ruling. They said no. They had determined the venture was too risky and the man's demands were too outrageous.

And so in January of 1492, the Genoese merchant Christopher Columbus saddled his mule and rode out of the west gate of Santa Fe alone, in defeat.

But all was not lost. His planning, wooing, and painstaking strategy had convinced many. As Columbus trotted away, the court was already in turmoil. Courtiers rushed to the throne to argue that the sailor's demands would be more than deserved if he really accomplished what he was proposing. And, more important, they contended that if Columbus succeeded in this quest and did so under the commission of another monarch, Ferdinand and Isabella would be humiliated in front of their friends and, worse, their enemies. The courtiers, it seemed, were believers, and their argument carried the day. The queen changed her mind and she sent a court messenger who overtook Columbus on a bridge near Pinos Puente. Bewildered and elated, the admiral-to-be turned his mule around and headed back to his destiny.

Christopher Columbus was by most accounts an imperfect and fallible hero, and yet by sheer force of will he took the world of the late Middle Ages and set it on its way to becoming the culture we inhabit today. Perhaps his greatest contribution lay not in his seamanship or even his grand vision, but in his ability to get others in the wheelbarrow.

It is our turn to follow in similar footsteps.

Why should you work to get people to believe in you and what you are trying to achieve? Because you are engaged in something important at work and with any luck it's something you really care about. To have any hope of succeeding, you need to get others *all in*.

We hope that this book has shown you that there is great power in building a culture where people believe. As the research and case studies have illustrated, it's a strategy that some of the best managers in the world are using to great effect. There is no question that the worldwide workforce has hidden reserves of ingenuity and resolve that can be tapped, and when all the elements for building a positive culture are at play, there is no question that work becomes not only more fruitful but a good deal more fun and satisfying.

And keep in mind that these powerful methods can be applied outside of the office as well, for the betterment of a nonprofit, community, school, or family. Wherever you decide to build a positive culture in this world that is so often dominated by mediocrity and apathy, you will find that you are able to create for others a future that is irresistibly bright.

Appendix

The Culture Works Process for Building and Sustaining a High-Performance Culture

Building upon extensive research into the key elements of the most profitable and sustainable cultures, we have developed a process that we've used with organizations worldwide to enhance employee commitment and drive real business results.

A brief overview of the Culture Works Process is below.

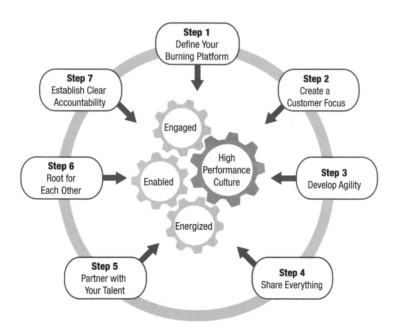

This is not a lockstep system but a path that is intended to include some interesting detours. After all, following the exact process used by Southwest Airlines, Starbucks, Apple, or Zappos is not likely going to fit your bank, hospital, or restaurant. The specific process of identifying, enhancing, and embracing culture is unique for every organization. However, this model and its accompanying exercises can serve as a pathway that will keep you focused and impact the probability of increasing not only employee commitment but business outcomes and company value.

You'll find in the model a progression that any manager of a large or small organization can use. An individual manager should start with a team assessment of strengths, weaknesses, opportunities, and threats (SWOT) and his or her team's level of E + E + E. The manager would then proceed through the seven steps to driving high performance, placing greatest emphasis on areas where improvement is needed.

However, if you are a leader of a large organization or if you have responsibility for cultural efforts at a corporate level, it may be interesting to note the process we use at The Culture Works when asked by company leaders to embark with them on a culture- or brand-improvement effort. We typically follow these steps:

1. Evaluate. Baseline measurements, interviews, and focus groups are used to assess current levels of employee engagement, enablement, and energy, and specific areas of the seven steps where we might place greater emphasis (the low-hanging fruit, if you will). By engaging key people in open, honest, and positive discussions around their perceptions of the organization's strengths, weaknesses, and opportunities, you can begin to see your blind spots and identify areas of potential growth.

2. Plan. With assessment report in hand, we work with leaders to define the core personality of the desired culture and through our system create a detailed plan that will lead you through the steps of the cultural-enhancement process. In this phase we develop milestones for each step of the process and accountability tools for managers to mark progress according to the strategy.

3. Communicate and train. Using a mixture of storytelling; recognition; social media; print, verbal, and video messages; lectures; and online and classroom workshops, the process of continuous learning begins. This includes weaving cultural-improvement efforts into performance evaluations, executive communication, accountability measures, and so on. It's one thing to hang up a poster of your values, but true culture change doesn't happen until you massage your principles into real behaviors expected of frontline employees who interact with your clients every day.

4. Reassess. Department-by-department analysis is conducted through employee and customer pulse or formal surveys. Areas of improvement are identified and addressed. And since very few cultural efforts reach 100 percent saturation on the first try, refinements to the entire program can be made at this point.

The questions at the root of any cultural-improvement effort are these: What do my customers want in our brand? And why would my employees care about this culture and live that brand?

Answers will come as you help each employee understand how their performance affects not only themselves but their teammates and the overall company, customers, community, and shareholders. Whether an employee is a frontline worker, a midlevel leader, or a senior executive, they should have clear and actionable definitions of performance that support the company's mission, core values, goals, and individual expectations.

Perhaps the best way to understand how we help all employees first become aware of and then internalize cultural expectations is through the 10/20/70 learning model:

- 10 percent of all learning happens during a formal training, communication, or event. (This is an important component, but not a fix-all. This is where most companies unwisely spend the bulk of their culture investment, and most usually stop here.)
- 20 percent of all learning happens from working directly

with your manager or role models. (In a cultural-improvement effort this is a coaching phase, helping managers and supervisors learn the language and behaviors that support your culture and brand, so they in turn can help their people. You will also develop cultural ambassadors where it matters most—in your leadership ranks, and by enlisting influential line managers and individual contributors.)

- 70 percent of learning occurs during real-life on-the-job experiences or individual cultural encounters. (This phase includes a heavy emphasis on reaching individuals where they work and providing clear tools, processes, and feedback mechanisms that educate, support, and acknowledge their vital work of supporting your clients.)

As you can see, a system-wide cultural initiative must gather a real head of steam to reach into all corners of the organization, and that takes time and commitment. But the simpler lesson for every manager is this: By using the process we have described in this book, you truly can find hidden reservoirs of ingenuity and drive in your teams. You can be the inspiration. The leaders and companies we have profiled have shown you how.

Visit TheCultureWorks.com for more tools and ideas.

Notes

Unless otherwise sourced in the notes below, the case studies in this book were compiled from hundreds of hours of firsthand interviews we conducted with employees and executives in the featured companies. The Towers Watson findings originated from our meetings with members of the company's senior research team and from their tireless work to find us interesting data. The notes that follow are organized by chapter. If a source is noted and appears again in a later chapter, it is acknowledged in the book's text but not sourced a second time in the notes.

Chapter 1. Get in the Wheelbarrow

For documentation on the Great Blondin we used the following sources: "Walking Distance," *Smithsonian* magazine, June 2009; "Niagara Falls, Waterfall," *Columbia Electronic Encyclopedia,* 6th ed., 2010; and the website tourniagara.com.

The quote from John F. W. Rogers was found in a September 1, 2011, *Businessweek* article, "Meet John F. W. Rogers, Goldman's Quiet Power Player," by William Cohan. It was cited there from a 2006 Harvard Business School case.

Stephen Sadove was quoted by Adam Bryant in "For the Chief of Saks, It's Culture That Drives Results," *New York Times,* May 29, 2010.

John Kotter and James Heskett's research was published first in their book *Corporate Culture and Performance,* reprint edition (New York: Free Press, 2011), and summarized in Kotter's February 10, 2011, column in *Forbes,* "Does Corporate Culture Drive Financial Performance?"

Eric Flamholtz's research was published in his article "Corporate Culture and the Bottom Line," *European Management Journal* 19, no. 3.

This research on complaining employees was derived from a Badbossology.com survey sponsored by Development Dimensions International and found in an article titled "Complaining About a Bad Boss Is a Big Time Drain" on the Badbossology website. The survey found the majority of employees spend ten hours or more a month complaining about or listening to others complain about bosses, while nearly a third spend twenty or more hours; we took the liberty of averaging that to 15.

The Gallup Organization data on the percent of not engaged and disengaged employees comes from Jennifer Robison, "Despite the Economy, Employees Remain Engaged," *The Gallup Management Journal,* January 14, 2010.

The quote from Rosabeth Moss Kanter is from Jim Kouzes and Barry Posner, *The Encouraging the Heart Workbook* (New York: Pfeiffer, 2010).

Chapter 2. The Belief Factor

Andrew Newberg's ideas are outlined in his book *Why We Believe What We Believe* (New York: Free Press, 2006).

We read first about the Saddam Hussein research in Sharon Begley, "Lies of Mass Destruction," *Newsweek,* Aug. 25, 2009; then through the article by Monica Prasad, Andrew Perrin, Kieran Bezila, Steve Hoffman, Kate Kindleberger, Kim Manturuk, and Ashleigh Smith Powers, "There Must Be a Reason: Osama, Saddam, and Inferred Justification," in *Sociological Inquiry* 20, no. 10 (2009).

The Republic by Plato has been published numerous times, perhaps most recently by Simon & Brown, 2011.

Detail on Bruce Lee was gleaned from the books *Tao of Jeet Kune Do* (Valencia, CA: Black Belt Communications, 1975); and John

Little's *Bruce Lee: The Art of Expressing the Human Body* (New York: McGraw-Hill, 1998); as well as the HistoryLink.org article "Lee, Bruce, (1940–1973): Martial Arts Master and Film Maker," by Alyssa Burrows, October 21, 2002.

Michael Phelps story includes information from the books *No Limits: The Will to Succeed,* by Phelps and Michael Abrahamson (New York: Free Press, 2009); and *Beneath the Surface* by Phelps, 2nd ed. (Sports Publishing LLC, 2008). The quote from Deborah Phelps comes from thesykesgroup.com, "Five Secrets to Creating a 'Goal' Medal Life (How Michael Phelps Can Help You Achieve Your Goals!)," by Ed Sykes.

We use two primary sources for the Howard Schultz references. The first is notes taken at a meeting we attended on March 30, 2011, at the Florence Gould Hall Theater in New York, where Schultz addressed *Inc.* magazine's Business Owners Council; the second is Schultz's book *Onward: How Starbucks Fought for Its Life Without Losing Its Soul* (Emmaus, PA: Rodale, 2011). The equity increase is a calculation from a five-year share price graph of SBUX at Yahoo Finance.

The Harvard study of obesity was reported by Nancy Hellmich in *USA Today,* "Obesity Is Contagious Among Friends," on November 9, 2010.

Chapter 3. E + E + E

We found the Research in Motion letter at BGR.com in "Open Letter to BlackBerry Bosses: Senior RIM Exec Tells All as the Company Crumbles Around Him," by Jonathan Geller, June 30, 2011. As we say in the book, the letter is allegedly from an executive at the company and we are relying on BGR to have verified its validity.

While the Chick-fil-A story comes almost exclusively from first-hand interviews, we did use some background from Chuck Salter's article "Chick-fil-A's Recipe for Customer Service" on FastCompany.com.

Chapter 4. Define Your Burning Platform

Quotes for the story about General Motors came from the program "403: NUMMI," *This American Life,* Chicago Public Media, distributed by Public Radio International, March 26, 2010; Sharon Silke Carty, "Seven Reasons GM Is Headed to Bankruptcy," *USA Today,* June 2, 2009; and James Risen, "GM Profit Up 42 Percent in Quarter," *Los Angeles Times,* February 4, 1986.

Information on Survival Anxiety was gleaned from Edgar Schein's article "The Anxiety of Learning—The Darker Side of Organizational Learning," in the Harvard Business School Archive, April 15, 2002.

Brad Garlinghouse's missive was covered in *The Wall Street Journal* on November 18, 2006, in an article entitled, "Yahoo Memo: The Peanut Butter Manifesto."

Background on Lincoln Electric came from the Harvard Business Publishing case study "Lincoln Electric Co." by Norman Fast and Norman Berg, 1975, revised July 29, 1983; and Jordan Siegel and Barbara Zepp Larson, "Labor Market Institutions and Global Strategic Adaptation: Evidence from Lincoln Electric," *Management Science 55,* no. 9 (September 2009).

John Sculley was quoted in the PBS television documentary *The Triumph of the Nerds,* 1996.

The quote from Jim Kouzes and Barry Posner is from their book *The Leadership Challenge,* 4th ed. (New York: Jossey-Bass, 2008).

Chapter 5. Create a Customer Focus

Peter Cohan's findings were published in his column in *Daily Finance,* "After 101 Years, Why GM Failed," on May 31, 2009.

Vijay Govindarajan's work can be found in his book *The Other Side of Innovation: Solving the Execution Challenge* (Cambridge, MA: Harvard Business Press, 2010); but we first found a summary of his ideas through Rick Newman's article in *US News & World*

Report, "10 Great Companies That Lost Their Edge," August 19, 2010.

Paul Quinn on PeoplePulse.com.au reported the research from TARP in the column "The Customer Complaint Iceberg."

The quote from Dave Frankland of Forrester Research came from the article "8 Ways to Listen to Your Customers" by Bianca Male, June 2, 2010, on the website BusinessInsider.com. It is purely a coincidence that we also wrote about eight ways to develop a customer focus, though we did read Male's article and there are great tips there.

Mark Zuckerberg's citation came from Miguel Helft, "For Buyers of Web Start-ups, Quest to Corral Young Talent," *New York Times,* May 17, 2011.

Marc Andreessen's quote was found in the book *Mavericks at Work: Why the Most Original Minds in Business Win,* by William Taylor and Polly LaBarre (New York: HarperPerennial, 2008).

Chapter 6. Develop Agility

For the story of Yuri Gagarin and John F. Kennedy, we read the books *Explorers,* Andrea De Porti (Buffalo, NY: Firefly Books, 2005); *Vostok 1,* Michael D. Cole (Springfield, NJ: Enslow Publishers, 1995); *The First Men in Space,* Gregory P. Kennedy (New York: Chelsea House Publishers, 1991); and *John F. Kennedy: A Biography,* Michael O'Brien (New York: St. Martin's Press, 2005).

The Jim Collins citation was from his book *Good to Great* (New York: HarperCollins, 2001). While we did challenge an idea from Collins's book, we in no way denigrate the importance of his overall work. The point we make is that scant attention is paid to consciously addressing the ideas of agility and change in the mainstream business press, but this turbulent economy has made it essential.

The background on agility from Lehigh University was found in the white paper "Agility and Flexibility: What's the Difference?" by

John Baker, May 1996, Cranfield School of Management, Cranfield University, UK.

Steve Jobs references came from a *Washington Times* column by Terry Ponick, "Steve Jobs: Visionary Revolutionary," October 8, 2011; and from "Pixar Founding Documents," Alvyray.com, retrieved April 19, 2010; and the financial report that Pixar averages the highest gross per release is from Wikipedia, which claims the statistic originated with Box Office Mojo.

The University of Pennsylvania Behavioral Health Corporate Services data came from PennBehavioralHealth.org and an article entitled "Stress." The piece sources a paper from the National Mental Health Association: "Stress—Copying with Everyday Problems."

The data on coronary bypass survivors and other information then cited to David Rock and Jeffrey Schwartz was found in their article in *strategy+business* entitled "The Neuroscience of Leadership," issue 43, summer 2006.

John Kotter's idea about effective general managers spending 80 percent of their time interacting with others was found on orgnet .com in a paper by Valdis E. Krebs entitled "Managing the Connected Organization." In the article "Winning at Change" in *Leader to Leader* No. 10 (Fall 1998), Kotter said, "Producing change is about 80 percent leadership—establishing direction, aligning, motivating, and inspiring people—and about 20 percent management—planning, budgeting, organizing, and problem solving."

The information on Hard Rock was primarily gleaned from firsthand interviews, but we did also cite Jeffrey Goldfarb's article "It's a Hard Rock Life," *American Way,* August 1, 2009.

Background on Rational AG came from the company's website and from an account related to us based on a tour by American business graduate students of the corporate headquarters in Landsberg am Lech, Germany.

The HP quote originated from Lew Platt, former chief executive of Hewlett-Packard, who observed, "If only HP knew what HP knows, we would be three times more productive." It was cited in a December 22, 2008, column on BusinessWeek.com by John Hagel and John Seely Brown entitled, "Harrah's New Twist on Prediction Markets."

Online forms of collaboration were reinforced in Tony Byrne's article "How to Use Internal Collaboration and Social Networking Technology," *Inc.* magazine, March 31, 2010.

Background on Big Blue's use of social media was courtesy Social MediaExaminer.com and Casey Hibbard's article "How IBM Uses Social Media to Spur Employee Innovation," February 2, 2010.

Chapter 7. Share Everything

The data on campaigning politicians and consumer trust levels in society was drawn from our book *Integrity Works,* written with Dana Telford (Layton, UT: Gibbs Smith, 2005). Original sources are cited in that work.

The data that only 36 percent of employees believe their leaders operate with integrity is from the book *The Speed of Trust* by Stephen M.R. Covey (New York: Free Press, 2008); the theory about why employees behave the way they do is from the paper "Behavioral Integrity as a Critical Ingredient for Transformational Leadership," in the *Journal of Organizational Change Management* 12, no. 2 (1999), by Tony Simons of Cornell University, and from Jim Kouzes and Barry Posner, who reported very similar findings in their book *Credibility: How Leaders Gain and Lose It, Why People Demand It* (New York: Jossey-Bass, 2003).

The research from John Schaubroeck, Simon Lam, and Ann Chunyan Peng was published as the paper "Cognition-Based and Affect-Based Trust as Mediators of Leader Behavior Influences on Team Performance," in *The Journal of Applied Psychology* 96, no. 4 (July 2011).

The Interaction Associates survey was cited in the paper "2011 Leadership, Collaboration, and Trust Research Report" by Andy Atkins on the InteractionAssociates.com website.

The Google 20 percent time statistic is documented and then the merits are debated in E. B. Boyd, "Why Google's '20 Percent Time' Isn't Stemming Its Brain Drain," *Fast Company,* November 29, 2010.

Chapter 8. Partner with Your Talent

We quoted Kip Tindell from a segment entitled, "The Container Store's Employee-Focused Culture" on the program CBS News *Sunday Morning,* March 6, 2011.

The data that 76 percent of employees want a secure and stable position was from Towers Watson's "2010 Global Workforce Study: The New Employment Deal."

Chapter 9. Root for Each Other

Zappos was featured in our book *The Orange Revolution* (New York: Free Press, 2010).

The financial impact of recognition and the story of KPMG were profiled in our book *The Carrot Principle* (New York: Free Press, 2009). The Towers Watson data on recognition was from the paper "Turbocharging Employee Engagement" on TowersWatson.com.

The 65 percent statistic and other 2011 recognition data came from globoforce.com and the article "Globoforce Workforce Mood Tracker: The September 2011 Report."

Chapter 10. Establish Clear Accountability

We wrote about the "99 percent employee" in *The Carrot Principle.*

Background on the Old West came from *Death of a Gunfighter* by Dan Rottenberg (Yardley, PA: Westholme Publishing, 2008).

The American Spelling Book by Noah Webster was republished as *The Original Blue Back Speller* by Vision Forum in October 2003.

Chapter 11. Renewing Belief

Mark Hurd's departure and succession planning was written about by Michael Watkins in the article "How to Deal with the Sudden Loss of a CEO," *Businessweek,* Viewpoint, August 11, 2010.

While we primarily relied on firsthand interviews for the story of Real Salt Lake, we did use several sources to provide background on soccer in the United States, including Marco R. della Cava, "Why the United States Doesn't Take to Soccer," *USA Today,* July 7, 2006; the article "Rasmussen Reports: US Soccer Popularity," which we found on myfoxphilly.com; and Stanley Holmes, "Soccer: Time to Kick It Up a Notch," *Businessweek,* November 22, 2004.

Chapter 12. Fifty-two Ways to Get Your People All In

Sections of the Tastefully Simple Warehouse Declarations are used with permission of Tastefully Simple. Copyright © 2011.

The book *Difficult Conversations: How to Discuss What Matters Most* was written by Douglas Stone, Bruce Patton, Sheila Heen, and Roger Fisher, and the tenth-anniversary updated edition was published by Penguin in 2010.

Chapter 13. In the Company of Believers

To write the concluding story of Christopher Columbus, we read the books *Columbus and the Age of Discovery* by Zvi Dor-Ner (New York: William Morrow, 1991); and *America Discovers Columbus* by Claudia L. Bushman (Hanover: University Press of New England, 1992).

Acknowledgments

We owe our first debt of gratitude to our agent and friend Kevin Small, who encouraged us to finally put to paper all we had learned about culture. He helped shape this proposal—demanding fresh ideas—and leads our book distribution efforts with the skill of a battlefield tactician.

Some are arguing that the traditional publisher is becoming less relevant; we would heartily disagree. Our editor, Emily Loose, not only saw great promise in this subject but took our first meandering manuscript and over months of work helped us weave it into a narrative that now has clarity and focus. Emily is brutally honest and ruthlessly determined, while still being one of the world's truly lovely people. To Emily, Martha Levin, Suzanne Donahue, Dominick Anfuso, Chloe Perkins, and the entire team at Free Press and Simon & Schuster, we thank you for finding us and helping us reach so many people. In just five years, our two previous books with you have sold more than half a million copies around the world and have been translated into more than twenty languages. Wow.

We express deep appreciation to Patrick Kulesa, Iva Ros, and everyone at Towers Watson who allowed us access to the research quoted herein.

Special appreciation also goes out to our amazing clients and those companies that allowed us into their halls: To the American Express team that includes David Kasiarz, Jim Dwyer, Rebecca Winslow Booth, Ken Chenault, Jim Bush, Doria Camaraza, and the entire leadership and employee team in Fort Lauderdale. To First Niagara, including John Koelmel, Marlene Piche, Kate White, Greg Gilroy, Lisa DiStasio, Siobhan Smith, Brent Kelly, Deb Valenti, David Lanzillo, Darlene Peters, and to the entire brand and culture team. To Ingrid Lindberg at Cigna and the entire team there; and to Diane Goodman for introducing us to Cigna in the first place. To Real Salt Lake, including Bill Manning, Dave Checketts, Dell Loy Hansen, John Kimball, Devin Barlow, Patti Benson, Brett Fischer, Tara Kroeger, Sarah Navarre, Gina Crezee (and the Rio Tinto team), and many others. To Margie Lynch, David Works, Clay Wahl, and Nicole Ryan at Kmart. To Bart Kaericher, Dudley Poppins, Bobby Kutteh, and the team at Crothall. To Dr. Kevin Fleming of Grey Matters International. To Mark Servodidio and Carlos Aguilera of Avis Budget Group. To those at Chick-fil-A, including Dan Cathy, Andy Lorenzen, Tim Tassopoulos, and Polly Scott. To John Berisford. To Baptist Health System in Alabama, including Shane Spees, Don Stuckey, and Alan Bradford. To Stanley Hainsworth at Tether Inc. To Calum MacPherson and Alison McCue of Hard Rock International. To Rich Gorman, Kathleen Gonzalez, and Jason Bell of the U.S. Army's Family and MWR Command. To the Coffee Bean team of Mel Elias, Mark Lindstrom, Nicole Scott, Melissa Borrego, and Danielle Pollard. To Zappos, including Tony Hsieh, Rob Siefker, and Maura Sullivan. To those at Pitt County Memorial Hospital, including Brian Floyd and, at the time, Elizabeth Veliz. To Fullham Football Club's Robert Ordever and Alistair Mackintosh. To Jill Blashack Strahan, Joani Nielsen, Edgar Timberlake, and the team at Tastefully Simple. To Frank Martire and Lisa Sweeney of FIS. To Equitable Life & Casualty's Rick Bass. To Amanda Felts at Atlantis Resort at Paradise Island in the Bahamas. To Tom Fanning of Ability Beyond Disability and his amazing team. To Ted Fowler of Golden Corral. To Texas Health Presbyterian Hospital Dallas president Britt Berrett. To the Pets at Home team, including Matt Davies, Ryan Cheyne, and Andrew Blaney. To GJ Hart at California Pizza Kitchen. To Ryan Giles at LinkedIn. To Teresa A. Witt and the team at Ely Lilly. To Ann Rhoades at Jet Blue. To Jay Staggs and the team at Murphy Oil. To Craig Rothenberg and Hans Melotte at Johnson & Johnson. To Gary Hyman, Andrew Heath, and all the good people of Rolls-Royce Energy. Finally, much gratitude is owed to our business hero Scott O'Neil at Madison Square Garden.

We rely so much on our amazing team at The Culture Works, especially Steve Gibbons, who served as a critical reader and advisor, and Machele Taliaferro, who helped keep the phones ringing while we were squirreled away writing. We thank our development team of Todd Nordstrom, Matt Look, and Mike Meyers; our instructor Cheryl Hutchinson; and our videographer Christopher King. Thanks also to our publicist Mark Fortier for his brilliance in making noise; and to Glen Nelson, Todd Nordstrom, Christie Giles, Noreen Gibbons, and Scott Christopher for their ideas about the manuscript. Our appreciation to Jon Elton, Matt Elton, Richard Sheinaus, and Andrew Hahn who provide design expertise, and Ashley Smith and Ryan Smith on social media. Also to our accounting whizzes Mark Durham and Jaren Durham.

We must thank the CBS team, including Mark Zulli, Michael Wallace, Jonathan Clark, Steve Swenson, Pat Carroll, and Tim Scheld. In addition, to Chad Jones for background on oil field workers, and to Troy Coil who introduced us to the story of the Niagara Falls daredevil. To those who provided us with advice: Thanks to Dave Ulrich and Norm Smallwood, Greg Blonder, and Randy Hain. Thanks for the support to Ted Priestly at Holy Cross Soccer, Kevin Smith of State Farm, Doug Sohn of AMA, Debbie White of Crump Insurance, and Shawn Boyer of SnagaJob. We also thank our old friend Eric Lange and and our new friend Sol Adler at the 92nd Street Y; and Arshad Chowdhury and Steve Tynan at ClearGears.

And yet we owe our greatest debt of gratitude to our families—to Jennifer and Tony, to Heidi, Cassi, Carter, Brinden, and Garrett, for your patience and love.

Index

About the Authors

Internationally recognized workplace experts Adrian Gostick and Chester Elton are founders of the global training and consulting firm The Culture Works, with a focus in recognition, teamwork, and culture. Learn more at TheCultureWorks.com.

Adrian Gostick is the author of numerous best-selling books on the workplace, including the *New York Times, USA Today,* and *Wall Street Journal* bestsellers *The Carrot Principle* and *The Orange Revolution.* His research has been called a "must-read for modern-day managers" by Larry King of CNN, "fascinating," by *Fortune* magazine, and "admirable and startling" by *The Wall Street Journal.*

Adrian's books have been translated into more than thirty languages and are sold in more than fifty countries around the world. As a leadership expert, he has appeared on numerous national television programs including NBC's *Today* show and has been quoted in dozens of business publications and magazines. Adrian earned a master's degree in leadership from Seton Hall University, where he is a guest lecturer on organizational culture. Visit his blog at adriangostick.com.

Chester Elton has been called the "apostle of appreciation" by *The Globe and Mail,* Canada's largest newspaper, and "creative and refreshing" by *The New York Times.* Chester is the coauthor of *The Carrot Principle* and *The Orange Revolution,* and his books have sold more than a million copies worldwide.

As a workplace expert, Chester has been featured in *The Wall Street Journal, The Washington Post, Fast Company* magazine, and *The New York Times,* and he appears in a weekly segment on CBS News Radio. A sought-after speaker and consultant, Chester has spoken to delighted audiences in Asia, Europe, and throughout North America. He works with firms such as American Express, Cigna, and Avis Budget Group. Visit his blog at chesterelton.com.

No matter the size of your team or the challenges you face, it is possible to build an All-In Culture.

Log in to receive the free tools that will help you and your team build and sustain high performance.

Visit **TheCultureWorks.com/Resources** for these free resources.

White Paper
Got a skeptic in your organization?
Get them a copy of our white paper
"Culture Eats Strategy for Breakfast."

Secrets of Winning Cultures
Chester Elton's 10 most popular CBS Radio podcasts–the surprising secrets of the world's most prestigious workplaces. Two-minute ideas that any manager can use to inspire belief at work.

Weekly Ideas in Your Inbox
The latest thinking on building a better workplace, sent weekly. Tips and tools every leader can use.

Films
Our cameras visited some of the remarkable cultures featured in this book–capturing real managers at work in some challenging environments. Learn how great leaders engage, enable, and energize their people.